How to Write
Your Novel

Books by Margaret Chittenden

DON'T FORGET TO DIE
DEAD BEAT AND DEADLY
DEAD MEN DON'T DANCE
DYING TO SING
AS YEARS GO BY
THE ENCHANTED BRIDE
WHEN THE SPIRIT IS WILLING
SHADOW OF A DOUBT
DOUBLE TAKE
THE WAINWRIGHT SECRET
THE SCENT OF MAGIC
THIS TIME FOREVER
UNTIL OCTOBER
FOREVER LOVE
BEYOND THE RAINBOW
FINDLAY'S LANDING
SONG OF DARK WATER
HOUSE OF THE TWILIGHT MOON
THE OTHER CHILD
FACE IN THE MIRROR

Writing as Rosalind Carson

THE MOON GATE
THE MARRYING KIND
CLOSE TO HOME
TO TOUCH THE MOON
LOVE ME TOMORROW
SUCH SWEET MAGIC
SONG OF DESIRE
THIS DARK ENCHANTMENT
LOVESPELL

Children's Books

WHEN THE WILD DUCKS COME HOME
MERRYMAKING IN GREAT BRITAIN
MYSTERY OF THE MISSING PONY

How to Write
Your Novel

► ► ►

by Margaret Chittenden

► ► ►

Publishers   The Writer, Inc.   *Boston*

Library of Congress Cataloging-in-Publication Data

Chittenden, Margaret.
    How to write your novel / by Margaret Chittenden.
    p. cm.
    ISBN 0-87116-178-8 (pbk.)
    1. Fiction—Technique. I. Title.
PN3365.C465 1995
808.3—dc20   95-35730
                                                   CIP

Printed in Canada

For my literary agent, Emilie Jacobson,
with affection, admiration, and gratitude

Contents

ACKNOWLEDGMENTS

My thanks to Stella Cameron, Margaret Carney,
and Kathleen Wolgemuth, who checked me out
and cheered me on.

Part I

PREPARATION

Introduction

When I was a very small child, I believed, sincerely and absolutely, that a lot of little people lived inside the radio. I believed that when you switched it off, they knew to stop talking.

As an adult, I still believe in all those little people, though now they live inside my head. I know they are there because they talk to me.

Many people hear voices. Some of them are called writers, and they spend days alone in rooms staring at the walls. It is the intent of this book to provide advice that will cut down on the amount of time you spend just staring at walls. Please note the word "advice." I cannot teach you how to write. I'm not sure anyone can. Any rules I could come up with would most likely be broken successfully by someone else. Somerset Maugham said, "There are three rules for writing the novel. Unfortunately, no one knows what they are."

What I *can* do is explain the techniques that work for me and might work for you. It is up to you to adapt, change, and tailor my advice as you develop your own methods for writing *your* novel.

Throughout, I will be including brief quotes from my own novels in order to illustrate various techniques. Mostly, I'm using my own work because I hesitate to analyze another author's writings. At least with my own, I know *why* I did whatever I did, and I don't have to worry about changing a word or phrase from the original if there's a reference to previous action that might be unclear.

This book is divided into two sections. Everything in Part One has to do with getting ready to write your novel. Part Two covers the actual writing. Each chapter (except Chapter Three) attempts to deal with one element of writing. It isn't actually possible, however, to separate these elements completely when plotting and writing a novel. When a writer works on a novel, he or she is constantly weaving back and forth between the plot and the characters and the setting. You can't put together a plot without taking its characters into consideration. Characters cannot grow without a plot in which to develop. A static description of setting can be boring.

I usually spend one or two months getting ready to write a novel and six to eight months on the writing itself. I have known writers who swear that as soon as they have an idea, they start writing the book. They don't know how it will all turn out or who will be in it until they actually write it. So they say.

If I attempted this approach, I'd be like the character in the Stephen Leacock story who "flung himself from the room, flung himself upon his horse, and rode madly off in all directions."

I'll admit I'm a fairly cautious individual. I wouldn't drive to a strange town without consulting a map. Nor would I build a house without a blueprint.

If you are quite sure you can write a novel without first developing characters and plot and setting, then feel free to jump to Part Two. Promise me, though, that if you don't finish your novel, or you do finish it but can't sell it, you'll read through Part One and at least *try* my advice.

Let us begin with a few maxims:

Maxim #1: Think positive. When I boot up my computer, a menu appears on the screen. It has a banner headline that reads, "I am a great writer." I typed this in there myself. I have discovered, you see, that my subconscious is a stickler for truth and justice; it wants above all else to keep me honest. So if I say to myself—or to someone else—well I'm not a very good writer, or I'm not good at plotting, or I can't write a synopsis, my subconscious takes out its hammer and chisel and carves in granite: "I'm not a good writer; I'm not good at plotting; I can't write a synopsis," and it makes sure that all those statements come true.

On the other hand, if I keep telling myself I'm a terrific writer, my subconscious tries to make that happen instead.

I want you to try this, right now. Just sit up straight, lift your chin, take a deep breath, let it out, and repeat after me, "I am a great writer."

Do this as often as possible, when you are alone. I would not advise you to go around doing it in public; if you do, people will run the other way when they see you coming. Just keep the knowledge of your greatness between you and your computer or typewriter or pen.

Maxim #2 (which is closely related to Maxim #1): Believe in yourself, within reason. While in the grip of creativity, I have been known to send up a prayer: *Please don't let me die until I get this wonderful book finished.* A writer needs that kind of ego. At the same time, a writer needs to face facts honestly and unflinchingly. This may *not* be the greatest story ever told.

Maxim #3: Don't give up. It is very easy to get discouraged when you are a writer. Rejection slips do not drop upon us as the gentle rain from heaven; they come at us sideways, arrows shooting straight through our hearts.

Most writers go through a rejection period before their work begins to be published. Some think when they start out that all they have to do is write something and send it out, and it will sell. I certainly thought so, though I wouldn't have expected to give a piano recital without practicing a few scales, and maybe learning to play "Twinkle, twinkle, little star," but I didn't apply such common sense to writing.

Rejection happens to everyone. My first children's book was turned down by twenty-four publishers before it sold. But it did sell. My first short stories were turned down by everybody. But eventually, after constantly honing and improving my work, I wrote a story an editor liked, and then another and another. Persistence pays.

Before I began to write novels, before I sold short stories to top magazines, I spent several years selling to Sunday school papers and trade magazines and Sunday newspaper magazines. I even sent a couple of short stories to a company that wanted to put stories into pie packages. (They were rejected.) I sent my manuscripts out over and over and over, and I always had about ten things out at a time, so if one came back I could still hope the other nine would sell. A writer needs a lot of hope.

I remember when all I wanted was to be published. *If I could just get one thing published.* Does that sound familiar? So I had an article published. *If I could just publish a short story.* O.K., I did that. *If I could publish a book, ah, then I'd be so happy*—which I was, except that I immediately wanted to do it again, and again, and again. Now I want each book to be better than the last. (And number one on *The New York Times* bestseller list wouldn't hurt!)

Belief in yourself as a writer isn't always easy to sustain. Writing is my career and my joy and my life, yet there are times when I sit in despair in front of my keyboard, convinced I can never again write anything that anyone would want to read. In spite of my profound belief in the power of positive thinking, I decide every other week that I'm not a real writer.

But then, suddenly, one of those little people starts talking in my head, and I start typing and it's going, I can feel it, the dam has broken, I've gone over the wall; metaphors are mixing, but it's going, it's going, and I am filled with a feeling of absolute glee. At such moments, I know I am a real writer after all.

How can you tell if *you're* a real writer? Well, if your hair is usually on end and your working uniform consists of grungy sweats or jeans, then you're probably a real writer.

If you "hear voices"; if words excite you, and you like to watch and think about people; if you neglect your family, discourage visitors, hardly ever write letters or remember birthdays; and if you don't worry too much about the dusting or dripping faucets—those are more clues.

Above all, real writers write. Which leads us to:

Maxim #4: Writers write. Regularly. Whether they feel like it or not. Whether they slept well the previous night, had a fight with their spouse or mother-in-law, are getting divorced or married, writers *write*.

Maxim #5: Take care of yourself. I have worked from 10 a.m. until 5 p.m. five days a week for many years now. I used to begin writing at 9 a.m. but then I realized running to the mailbox wasn't really enough physical exercise. A writer needs good health. So now I begin each day at the gym with workouts that keep me in shape and stimulate my brain.

Maxim #6: Take your work seriously. There's

no doubt about it, writing is work. In the course of creating a story or a novel, a writer can expend as much energy as a laborer. Sure, writing *looks* easy—which often makes it difficult to convince one's spouse, children, and neighbors that writing is work. It helps to let everyone know you will be working from 9 a.m. until noon, or from 6 p.m. until midnight, or every Saturday afternoon, whatever schedule works for you. Try to set regular hours, even if it's only one hour a day or two hours a week.

Maxim #7: Make a private place for yourself. I started out writing in a corner of my bedroom, graduated to a tiny den, then to a slightly bigger room, and now have a large office in my house with its own bathroom—luxury beyond imagining.

Don't do anything else in this private place except write. I'm a purist about this. My office space is sacrosanct; everything in it is dedicated to my work.

Maxim #8: Know what you write. I began writing in 1970. I would have started in 1968, but I attended a writers' conference and heard several established writers say, "Write what you know." I thought this was excellent advice, but unfortunately I didn't know *anything*. I pondered this problem for two years before it occurred to me that none of us comes into the world knowing anything; everything has to be learned. So I have amended the advice, "Write what you know," to "Know what you write." If you, too, feel you know nothing, be assured that you can learn almost anything.

Maxim #9: Write because you can't *not* write. (I know, I know, it isn't good English, but it says what I want it to say.) To be successful at writing you can't just mess around with it now and again. You have to look upon it as a vocation, a lifetime commitment. Above all, you have to love doing it.

In spite of all the people who live and talk and love and fight for space in a writer's head, writing is a lonely profession. Most writers sit alone in a room, hour after hour, day after day. As you read this book and work at becoming a published writer, I hope you will keep in mind that those of us who are fairly well established have all traveled the same lonely road, alternating between euphoria and despair. When you sit down to write, imagine me hovering benignly somewhere behind your left shoulder, saying, "You can do it. You can write."

There are many rewards that come from a successful writing career. People think of you as an interesting person. It's not all that likely, but it's even possible to become famous and wealthy. Most of us want to sell our writing—yes, writing is a business as well as an art and a craft—but money isn't necessarily our only motive. Many writers barely scrape by; yet they keep on writing year after year. Why? Because they love doing what they do, and they don't want to do anything else.

The truth is, you see, that no matter how far you climb in the writing world, no matter how much money you make, or how much critical acclaim you receive, when the glamorous aspects of the writer's life are over—the keynote speaking at conferences, the lunches with editors, the publishing parties, the talk shows, the newspaper interviews and the autograph parties—all that is left is the writing.

And the writing is everything.

◄ 1 ►

Perspiration and Inspiration

Here's the most important thing I ever learned about writing a novel: *You don't have to begin with an idea big enough to fill a whole book.* Until I understood this, I was unable to plot, paralyzed by the fear that I couldn't come up with an idea sensational enough.

A novel does not arrive in the writer's brain all at once. Like most forest fires, a novel usually starts from a tiny spark—a word, a sentence, a question, a wish, only occasionally a full-blown idea. Slowly, gradually, you add kindling to the spark—a character here, a situation there, a setting.

Mine is not the kind of mind that pops up ideas like bread out of a toaster. I write one or two books a year, which means I need only one or two ideas a year. Even those are hard to come by. Periodically, I have to root around in the attic of my mind to see if anything is lurking there.

These are some of the ideas I've started from:

1) Suppose there really were a perfume that would make a woman irresistible?
2) Is there anything to reincarnation?
3) I want to go to Bermuda.
4) I love to read English country-house murder mysteries. I wonder if I could write one.
5) Does an identical twin hate it when a person calls him or her by the other's name? Suppose the person were a lover?
6) I ought to do a ghost story, just for fun.
7) More than anything else, I would like to write a mystery series.
8) I've finished all my projects, and I don't have a contract for another. I'd better come up with an idea for a new novel!

Sometimes the spark of inspiration comes to me in the form of an image: I once told my husband jokingly that when I look in the mirror first thing in the morning, I often see my Aunt Ellie. (Aunt Ellie died many years ago.) Right away I thought, what if it *was* my Aunt Ellie in the mirror? This scary notion became a reincarnation novel titled *Forever Love.*

Watch for a spark passing through your mind. You might be half asleep in bed, or reading a book, gardening, dancing, taking a walk. . . . If you don't keep a sharp lookout, the idea will pass right on through without catching on fire. For me, at least, ideas are not only hard to come by, they are fleeting. If I don't write them down *immediately,* even if it's the middle of the night, I will remember only that I had an idea. I keep small notepads all over the house, and in my purse, pocket, and car. When I have a few minutes to spare, I type the notes into my computer.

Did you notice that I called an idea a spark of *inspiration*? In my opinion inspiration has received a lot of undeservedly bad press. For years writers have been brainwashed into believing Thomas Edison's statement, "Genius is one percent inspiration and ninety-nine percent perspiration."

I realize I'm criticizing a great inventor, but I think Edison should have taken a second look at his mathematics. I believe inspiration and perspiration have a symbiotic relationship, that one isn't much use without the other.

We all know that perspiration is important in any creative activity. There's an old German proverb that goes: "If I rest, I rust." Most of us have heard that if we want to be writers, or want to be better writers, we should select a fixed number of hours at a certain time of the day, or on a certain day of the week, and sit in a chair until we've written ten or fifteen or twenty pages. I've often suggested something like this myself. It's good advice. But sometimes it's taken to mean that there's no room for inspiration in a writer's life. This is far from the truth.

Let's look at the first of the sparks I mentioned above: "Suppose there really were a perfume that would make a woman irresistible?" This idea came to me while I was watching a TV commercial. As soon as I recognized that I was having an idea, I wrote it down. Eventually that "spark" became *The Scent of Magic*.

Once I've written the idea down, *I try very hard not to think about it*. There's a Spanish saying: "The procession marches inside you." Some time after experiencing that small spark, I realize there's a conversation going on in my head that has to do with the idea I had last night, or last week, or last year. Characters are talking to one another and to me, and I write down what they say, without worrying about who is talking or where all of this will fit in the novel. Most of it *will* fit, I've learned.

Don't try to think about the whole novel at first. Let your initial spark sputter to life in your subconscious. Make notes as ideas come to you. Don't worry where anything will go or what it means until you've got it all down. Give inspiration a chance.

Listen to this quote from Wolfgang Amadeus Mozart:

> When I am, as it were, completely myself, entirely alone, and of good cheer—say, traveling in a carriage or walking after a good meal or during the night when I cannot sleep—it is on such occasions that my ideas flow best and most abundantly.

Mozart is talking about inspiration. His inspiration wouldn't have meant much to him if he hadn't put in a lot of hours practicing his violin and studying music with his father—which is *per-*

spiration—but his music wouldn't be nearly as thrilling without his *inspiration*.

An engineer once wrote that he had been trying very hard to solve a certain problem without success and was developing a fear of failure. Then one day, as he was riding on a crowded bus, mulling over personal matters, the solution to the problem came to him in a flash. The solution would not have come to him if he hadn't formerly been working very hard to solve the problem, but would it have come to him at all if he hadn't taken a little holiday from thinking about that particular problem?

I recall a television interview in which playwright Neil Simon compared an idea to a ball in a pinball machine. Isn't that a wonderful image? Can you see that ball ricocheting around in your brain, lighting up various areas as it strikes a response?

We all have our own ways of developing ideas. I live in a resort area that is two hours by car from the nearest large city. About twice a month, my husband and I drive to the city for a day of shopping and appointments. Quite often on these jaunts we discover we've gone a hundred miles without saying more than a dozen words.

During the journey, I don't consciously *think* about my work. Mostly I vegetate. And things come to me. I may suddenly think of the solution to a problem in the plot I'm currently working on. Or one of the voices in my head introduces me to a new character. A scene appears, complete with setting and dialogue. I write down everything that occurs to me. All of this comes under the heading of inspiration.

I think that many writers concentrate too much on the perspiration aspect of our craft. I have seen writing programs that are designed as blueprints for fiction. Some have grids and squares to fill in before you begin to write. I've read articles and heard speeches that insist you must allot a certain number of pages for the beginning, another number for the end; your turning point must come exactly in the middle; you must have a summary at the end of every scene; and you mustn't think of writing until you know the story question—and its answer—and on and on.

These systems always sound marvelous to me, but they affect me much the same way as advertisements for wrinkle cream do. Even though I *know* they aren't going to work for me, I can't resist trying them. They have supposedly proved to be successful for other writers. (They might even work for you, and if they do I'd like to hear from you.) Unfortunately, when I try to do them my stomach gets tied in knots, and I do not come up with anything remotely creative.

I think if I followed these blueprints, I'd end up with something that reads like a paint-by-number kit applied to words. I cannot believe it's possible to create something new and original from a programmed formula.

Several years ago, I read about a man who was designing a computer program that would write soap opera scripts. He was asked if the program would ever be able to write stories as creative as those by a writer. And he gave a great answer: He said the program would get you fourteen *clones* of *Star Wars,* but it wouldn't get you *Star Wars.*

It seems to me that if we write by number we will produce novels that look and sound like the novels other people are writing by number. There is, after all, a lot more to writing than typing.

If, on the other hand, we write from the primordial soup of information that we have in our own heads—the things we have observed, or learned, or heard, or suffered from or worried about—we will surely come up with something different, something interesting, something that might even be wonderful.

I don't mean to suggest that the advice in these various plotting systems is wrong or misguided. I can read them and say, "Yes, I do this and that, and I have this and I wrap it all up like that." However, I don't think about any of it before I start.

Mostly, I turn my creative mind loose and let it ramble and stumble and groan. Only when I have my storyline safely stored in my computer and on a floppy disk and on my tape backup (I'm paranoid) do I check to make sure my characters have goals, that I have enough suspense, that the conflict is strong, and the story is believable—but only *after* I've written my first sloppy but inspired draft.

Perspiration. Inspiration. Sometimes one comes first, sometimes the other.

Albert Einstein said he discovered the theory of relativity by picturing himself riding on a ray of light. That's inspiration. Backed by perspiration. I could picture myself riding on a ray of light for the rest of my life, and I wouldn't come up with the theory of relativity, because I don't have Einstein's background in mathematics and physics, and I certainly don't have his brain.

At the same time, I can identify with Einstein. If I hadn't exuded perspiration from taking courses and studying dozens of books on creative writing and reading hundreds of novels to see how writers do the magical things they do; and if I hadn't learned all I could of English grammar and spelling, I would not come up with material for a readable novel.

On the other hand, although I have a regular routine, I also take the time to go for long walks on the beach so that I can listen to what's going on inside my head. If my work isn't going well, I lie down and gaze at the ceiling, until my imagination starts working again.

If *you* suddenly feel like Wile E. Coyote, air-walking off a cliff over an abyss, legs churning like propellers, don't panic, just take a break. Sooner or later, your characters will start talking to you again, and you can rush back to your writing area and go to work.

If all else fails, take a tip from H.G. Wells: "If you are in difficulties with a book, try the element of surprise: Attack it at an hour when it isn't expecting it."

Try three o'clock in the morning. I've had some of my most creative ideas then. Insomnia is a writer's best friend.

Some writers have had very definite ideas about the environments they need to encourage inspiration. Samuel Johnson liked to have a purring cat, some orange peel, and a cup of tea with him when he wrote.

Dickens turned his bed to the north so the magnetic forces would help him create. Kipling had to have black ink. Proust insisted on a soundproof room. Beethoven poured cold water over his head to stimulate his brain. (I would suggest you don't try this while seated at your computer or electric typewriter.)

In addition to an ergonomically designed chair and keyboard, a desk that is the right height, and a foot rest, my working environment includes my trips to the city, walks on the beach, and sessions of staring at the ceiling. You must find the stimuli that work for you. Perspire. Get inspired. Write.

◄ 2 ►

Thinking It Through

Now that you are inspired, it's time to start thinking *consciously* about your story idea. If your subconscious has been providing all kinds of interesting bits and pieces but now the spark seems to have dimmed and the whole project is sitting like a lump in your brain, employ painter Jasper Johns' famous rule for making art: "Take an object. Do something to it. Do something else to it."

You might nudge it with a few questions, such as the standbys of reporting: *who, where, what, when, why,* and *how*?

What kind of novel is this? Most writers start out by writing the kind of books they like to read. A writer can belong to any race or ethnic background, may be young or old, rich or poor, male or female, thin or fat, tall or short. But one thing all writers have in common is a lifelong love of reading.

Don't worry if you can't decide right off what kind of novel you want to write. Just keep the question in mind and try to answer it before you get too far along.

Often, when I ask a new writer what kind of novel he or she is writing, the answer I get is "mainstream." Many writers seem reluctant to acknowledge a preference for writing in any particular category. I don't know why. Whether hardcover or paperback, so-called literary, popular, or mainstream, a novel is usually classifiable as a mystery, thriller, romance, fantasy, action-adventure, western, horror or science fiction novel. (I say *so-called* literary, popular, or mainstream, because I dislike the implication that you can't have one without the other.)

If you *can* determine what kind of novel you are writing, your plotting tasks are simplified. (This doesn't mean the plotting is ever easy.) Once you decide on the kind of novel—mystery, romance, etc.—try to classify it further. If it's a mystery, is it a "cozy," like most of Agatha Christie's? A cozy would not feature a lot of overt violence, though violence certainly triggers every mystery plot. Is it "hard-boiled"? Traditionally, a mystery novel— as written by Raymond Chandler, Ross Macdonald, and the like—starred a male detective, often a private investigator (P.I.), who was not afraid to get down and dirty with the crooks he had to confront. Now the hard-boiled mystery novel is becoming inhabited by an increasing number of tough *female* detectives: Marcia Muller's Sharon McCone; Sara Paretsky's V.I. Warshawski; Sue

Grafton's Kinsey Millhone, and a growing number of others.

Is your novel more likely to be a police procedural, similar to Ed McBain's well-known stories about the 87th Precinct? Or might you consider a historical police procedural, such as those written by Anne Perry?

How about espionage? A woman-in-jeopardy suspense story? The more specifically you can identify your novel, the easier it is to plot it.

If you are writing a mystery, you're going to need a murder victim. Who will it be? What kind of sleuth would you prefer? Male, female, amateur, professional, police, private, young, old, middle-aged; gay or straight; American, African American, Hispanic, British, Chinese, Norwegian. . . all of these appear in today's crime novels.

Every decision you make moves your plot forward.

If you decide to write a romance novel, you can break this category down into many types: sweet romance, sensual romance, erotic romance, romantic suspense or intrigue, romantic adventure, contemporary or historical or regency or western. Will your novel feature time-travel, like the novels of Constance O'Day-Flannery or Jack Finney; paranormal elements such as Linda Lael Miller's Vampires; or will it take place in an alternate world, like Marilyn Campbell's Innerworld series? The list goes on. There are many excellent writers in all of these genres. Talk to your bookseller. Read widely. Determine which type of novel interests you.

For a romance, you'll need a hero and a heroine. You'll need occupations for them, and a problem that will keep them apart emotionally, though not physically. You can't have much of a romance if the two people never see each other. A logger hero who favors unlimited timber-cutting and a heroine who is an avid environmentalist would have a problem getting together, even if they were strongly attracted to one another. A man who divorced his wife for adultery would be wary of a woman who appears to be a flirt.

You'll need to decide whether hero or heroine has been previously married, if either one has children. For a paranormal novel, you'll require a ghost or a vampire or whatever ghoulie you can dream up.

The science fiction umbrella covers "hard" nuts-and-bolts science fiction, featuring much extrapolation. This category may also include speculative fiction—other worlds, other cultures, distant planets.

In writing science fiction, you have to decide if you're going to write about technological developments or interstellar pirates, in this century or some future century, or a book like Neal Stephenson's *The Diamond Age,* which bows to both past and future, depicting a culture in which neo-Victorian dress and attitudes prevail, but set in a future dominated by nanotechnology.

The type of science fiction story you choose will

influence your choice of characters—and vice versa.

Fantasy novels, which deal with magic and superstition involving mythical creatures—wizards, trolls, and dragons—are enjoying great popularity today. Robert Jordan's multivolume epic fantasy, *The Wheel of Time*, is a fine example of this genre.

Horror novels, like those by Stephen King, Dean Koontz, and John Saul, differ in their approaches, but all of them appeal to tremendous numbers of readers.

Whatever type of novel you want to write, it is important that you first read widely in the field to find out what has been done, what is being done. Join whichever writers' organization focuses on your kind of novel, talk to librarians and booksellers to learn as much as you can about past and present trends, then write fresh, original stories that come out of your brain and heart and soul.

Question: Why should you decide early what kind of book you are writing?

Answer: When you make *any* decision about your novel, you are beginning to plot.

When my questioning and prodding stop producing answers, I turn to research, which is one of the greatest aids to me in plotting a novel. Whenever I talk about research, I remember the historical novelist who sat next to me on a panel at a writers' conference years ago. Knowing that I (then) wrote only contemporary fiction, she expressed surprise that I was on the panel. "What on earth do you have to research?" she asked.

I research everything that has to do with my story settings and background, including characters' occupations, interests, and hobbies. In writing a mystery, I interview police experts and research various murder weapons and methods.

I'm always on the lookout for unusual occupations. If I meet a marine biologist at a party, I'll pin him to the wall until I've learned all I can about his field. A medical examiner would be lucky to escape my clutches within a week. Most people like to talk about their professions or occupations, and are usually flattered by a writer's interest in them. I've never been turned down when I ask for an interview with a practicing professional in any field. My usual approach is to tell the expert that I'm eager to depict his job, area of expertise, requirements of the career, and so on, as accurately as possible.

I always *write* ahead to request an interview, because a letter is less intrusive on the person's time than a telephone call; after the person has agreed by letter to an appointed time, I follow up with a phone call or visit. I prepare carefully for the interview with a list of questions. I dress appropriately—a suit or tailored dress for a police station, corporate headquarters or embassy; jeans, shirt, and sneakers for a wildlife control officer who has promised to take me out in his boat to look at beaver lodges. I don't interrupt my expert while he is talking with stories of my own.

I don't stay too long. I thank him or her, and I write a thank-you letter afterward.

Some writers do all their research by reading. I also read a great deal on the various subjects I want to deal with in my fiction. I recently wrote a novel that took place in part during World War II. I read at least six books that covered far more than the information I needed, but my reading gave me a definite feel for the period.

A writer must never stop learning. If you don't keep putting ideas and information into your brain, you won't have anything to bring out. I buy an enormous number of books and subscribe to a lot of magazines, adding a few and dropping others every year. Right now I get *New York Magazine, Self, Nutrition, Country Guitar* and *The Smithsonian,* as well as various writers' magazines and the local newspaper of whatever place I am currently writing about.

I have taken courses in business management, psychology, French, Japanese, and self-defense, among others. What is my motivation for all this self-improvement? *There might be a book in it.* Magic words, as far as I'm concerned.

Because I write mysteries, police work fascinates me. I've gone to every lecture in my own and in neighboring states that had anything whatsoever to do with police procedure or law enforcement or forensics.

But I don't concentrate only on police work. Over the years I have joined several organizations that deal with the arts, with music, with the study of wine. About the time these organizations are getting ready to elect me to an office, I quit, having learned as much as possible.

In addition to all of this, I travel quite a bit. My initial idea for a novel often *starts* with place. When I decide on a place as the setting for a novel, I try to go there if at all possible. I've been to Quebec City, London, Paris, Cornwall, Bermuda, Tokyo, and many states in the U.S.—all in search of a story, because I believe that stories are waiting for me in every interesting town or country I've ever wanted to visit.

When it's not possible to research stories on the spot, I turn to other sources of information. I might start with my local library and college libraries. Make a friend of your reference librarian—he or she is always able to suggest sources of research material. Check out books that deal with your chosen areas, and research *The Readers' Guide to Periodical Literature* for magazines that cover your setting, the occupations of your characters, and so forth. Don't rely on only one reference book or article—read several; you'll find they don't always agree. It's *never* a good plan to depend on other people's fiction for your research. Who knows how thoroughly those novelists checked their "facts"?

Talk to local booksellers—they are usually extremely knowledgeable—and travel agents, who have access to information about areas all over the world. Often I begin with travel guides to a certain area, then zero in on sources listed in them—tourist information offices (they are always delighted to send brochures, maps, accommodation information), police departments, historical societies, chambers of commerce, local magazines and newspapers available by subscription. Look through the magazines and newspapers for video advertisements; videos will bring you not only the sights of your chosen place, but the sounds.

Newspapers are among my favorite resources. If your local library has facilities for reading microfilm, request interlibrary loans of microfilms of foreign and American newspapers, dealing with whatever place or historical period you are interested in.

If you *can* manage to go to the place you are interested in, the benefits of live research are enormous. While I'm driving or walking the streets and alleys or country lanes of my chosen spot, talking to the inhabitants, eating *pâté de foie gras* or fish and chips or *oyako dombori,* my story assembles itself in my mind. I read the local newspapers; photograph or video the buildings, scenery, flora and fauna; buy postcards, local books, maps; pick up every brochure I can find, including the ones provided by hotels—"This Week In . . ." theater guides, shopping guides, anything I think might be useful. I make notes constantly, watching and listening and yes, eavesdropping. Things happen to me. I write them down. They may become part of the story. It seems as though the sheer weight of the material I gather forces a storyline to surface.

When I was doing book research before a trip to Japan, I read this statement: "On the Shinkansen (bullet train) between Tokyo and Kyoto, refreshments are served." I made a note of this. When I traveled on that same bullet train, I discovered how that terse statement translated in real life. Refreshments were served by several sweet-faced young women who paraded the aisles with hand-carts, chanting in voices like wind chimes, "*Cannedu* [canned] juice, *cannedu* beer, sandwichi, *ikaga-desuka* [how about it?]"

Doesn't that seem more interesting than "refreshments are served"?

I have also found several stories in my own backyard. I just had to go out and study it with the eyes and ears and nose of a writer. I "hunted and gathered" in exactly the same way I do in other states or countries. While working on one novel, I took a ferry to a nearby island fourteen times before the sky was clear enough for me to see exactly how the mountains looked from a certain part of the island. It would be clear when I started out, but halfway there, haze obscured the view. This in itself became part of the story.

Research can be helpful in other ways, especially if you are planning a novel that is a little out of the ordinary. Some time ago I wrote a couple of novels that dealt with reincarnation. As part of my preparation, I visited a psychic who helped me regress hypnotically to my "former" lives, at the same time tape-recording everything I said in our four fairly long sessions. I used almost all of this material in the novels. Painless research. Painless plotting.

In preparing to write a mystery series set on the San Francisco Peninsula, I made four trips to the area. I read guidebooks, articles about local trees, flowers, the weather. I did a lot of research on earthquakes and police procedure and forensic medicine, and interviewed several police experts. The series features a country-western bar, so I've visited several and read about others. I even studied line dancing and bought a cowboy hat and boots.

Whether you do your research in books, magazines, or on the spot, be sure you amass enough background material to form a solid basis for your novel. Saturate yourself with as much information as you can and make sure you study your subject enough to feel confident of your accuracy.

◄ 3 ►

Plot and Character: Inseparable Elements

I don't believe in organizing my material too much before I begin to write a novel, though I know very successful writers who make plot notes on green paper, characters on yellow, settings on pink. Others write all their notes on a series of index cards and shuffle them around until they have a storyline. Some put dividers in a three-ring binder and label them Characters, Situation, Plot, Setting, etc. Many writers do all their arranging and rearranging in the computer. All of these methods are workable. Only you can decide if they would work for you. They don't for me. My research materials go into a wine box that is about $14'' \times 14'' \times 12''$ deep.

When I decide I have enough material, I'm ready to begin developing characters and plot.

I used to worry a great deal about which to work on first, plot or characterization. Many writers say you should always begin with character. Others insist that you should always begin with plot. I've solved the dilemma for myself by refusing to separate these two elements. I start with my tiny spark—my idea—and I add to it bit by bit, without trying to classify or organize. As my characters grow, the plot develops; as the plot grows, the characters develop. In this way, the characters are shaped by their environment, and they in turn shape their environment... Which is the way life is, isn't it?

Of course, not all of my ideas work out. I'm going to talk only about the ones that do. But in the course of plotting a novel, I discard dozens of ideas before I find the one that works. For most writers, plotting involves a great deal of trial and error.

At this stage of my preparation, I spend hours digging into my box to find out what I have, and feeding it into my brain. And I discover, *always,* that something magical has happened to the notes, brochures, maps, photographs, magazines, menus, postcards, audio and video tapes and newspaper clippings that I have thrown into that box: They have *blended.* They have *fermented.* (I use a wine box, remember!)

Looking for the notes about the ways in which ghosts have been said to materialize, I come across a picture postcard of a Queen Anne Victorian house in Port Townsend, Washington, and my ghost magically acquires a Victorian gown complete with bustle and cheerfully goes off to haunt that very house—as it did in my novel *When the Spirit Is Willing.*

At the bottom of the box, I find the menu from

that great little restaurant I want my characters to go to, and I inadvertently pull out a *Country Living* magazine picture of a cottage with a picnic bench in its glorious flower garden. Now my plot takes another twist.

As I dig and read, ideas and snippets of ideas come to me. I may not know what I'm going to do with all of them, but I write them down, confident my subconscious will eventually work them into a storyline.

This is what the wonderful writer Madeleine L'Engle says on the subject:

> My writing knows more than I know. What a writer must do is listen to her book. It might take you where you don't expect to go. That's what happens when you write stories. You listen and you say "Aha," and you write it down. A lot of it is not planned, not conscious, *it happens while you're doing it.* [My emphasis.] You know more about it after you're done.

Yes.

Beginning work on *Shadow of a Doubt,* I came across a picture postcard of a glass-bottomed boat. Gazing at it, I remembered looking down at all the colorful fish in Bermuda's coral reef. And I thought, well, yes, someone could drown there. Perhaps everyone on the boat is looking through the glass bottom as the body goes down. They don't see anyone push the person overboard, so they think the victim's death is an accident, or suicide, but it's neither.

Right off I wondered, *who* is the person who

drowned? If the drowning is not an accident or suicide, then it must be murder. So *who* is the murderer? By the time I wrote down the possible answers to those questions, I had taken several plot and characterization steps.

Here's a concrete example of the freewheeling way I work back and forth on characters and plot, culled from the preparations I made for my novel *The Scent of Magic.*

The original idea suggested a perfume that would make a woman irresistible. As I began thinking *consciously,* I saw that making my heroine irresistible would mean that every man who saw her would want her, and her only recourse would be to hide in a cave for the rest of her life.

So I changed the initial idea to read: Suppose there were a perfume that would give a woman her heart's desire? At this point, I applied the five W's: *Who* is the woman? *Where* did she get the perfume? *When? Where* does the story take place? *What* kind of perfume is it? *Why* does she use the perfume?

While I was mulling these W's, discarding most ideas as fast as they came to me, a friend called and invited me to an antique show.

As soon as I walked in the door at the show and smelled that heady mixture of lemon oil, dust, rust, and mustiness that accompanies agglomerations of old stuff, I *knew* my heroine would acquire the perfume *here*; that she would be a dealer in vintage clothing; and that she would wear it to advertise her store. I could *see* her: Casey, a petite young woman with inquisitive green eyes, wearing her red hair in a Gibson-Girl style—a slightly old-fashioned young woman with conventional values, but with a contemporary mind of her own. I wrote all of this down and began researching the show, looking for characters, old perfume bottles, vintage clothing.

This may sound weird, but I believe that everything that happens to you and around you may have a place in the novel you are working on. Into *The Scent of Magic* went the film festival that was also taking place in town that week, along with an adventure I'd heard about that involved a young man and a stolen airport shuttle bus, and an article I read on landscape gardening, which became the hero's occupation.

As I plotted along on *The Scent of Magic,* I felt that the story was too frivolous. There's nothing wrong with stories written just to entertain, but I try to work in serious issues when I can. As it happened, when I was leaving a local department store one day, I saw a young white woman sitting outside on the ground, holding a baby and begging for money.

I talked to her and gave her what help I could, then put her into my novel, where she became Sarah, a pregnant African-American. (All real-life characters and situations change when you put them into your fiction—as they should.) Because I didn't want to portray any ethnic group as automatically disadvantaged, I added Skip, a very successful African-American restaurateur with a story of his own. He turned out to be Casey's best friend, and pretty soon he became involved with Sarah.

This will give you an idea of how I weave back and forth between plot and characters. Writers make a mistake, in my opinion, when they think of a plot as a long line stretching from the beginning to the end of a novel. I try to *build* a plot from the ground up, adding layers wherever I can. To keep a reader turning the page, you need several layers of plot, character, and suspense.

To add layers to characters, I ask myself where they originally came from, if their parents are alive, if they have brothers or sisters, if they grew up poor or wealthy. So the story grows, and the characters come to life. A storyline begins to emerge, and I start making notes for the plot in a fairly thick exercise book—the three-subject kind.

As the characters start walking around in my mind, I choose names that really fit them, using a baby-name book that gives the meanings and ethnic backgrounds of male and female names. (I also have some computer software that does the same thing.) When naming characters, keep in mind that no two should sound alike enough to be confusing to the reader. Recently, I watched a TV drama in which one character was named Randy and another Mr. Randolph. A novel I read had characters with names like Penelope, Paul, Mr. Preston, and Pamela, and I became thoroughly confused. It's never a good idea to confuse your reader.

I make a list of my characters' names as I come up with appropriate ones, including a *few* descriptive details. (I'll need many more details worked out before I begin to write—character quirks, mannerisms, gestures, habits, hobbies, education—but for easy reference I make a separate list to keep handy as I do the actual writing. In this way I not only avoid having names that sound alike, but I don't mistakenly refer to a blue-eyed person as a green-eyed person.)

Example:

Simon Hunter: 6'3", age 33, blue eyes, black hair, land developer.

Rebecca Penberthy, 5'9", light-brown eyes (don't forget she wears glasses), black hair, health store owner.

Clytie Belyar, medium height, young, West Indian, cockney accent, ethnic clothing, pub owner.

I try always to come up with interesting names. You might expect Clytie Belyar, I think, to be colorful, and possibly eccentric, rather than boring. Rebecca Penberthy is a Cornish woman, so she has a Cornish name.

Quite often, I change the name of one or more people once I get into the writing, always referring to my list of names before making the change. Once the story people start moving and talking and breathing, I might even change the color of a character's hair or eyes if some of the characterizing details don't quite fit. Anything can be changed as long as the changes are consistent with the character.

Plot and characterization take giant steps forward when I decide on my characters' occupations. That's when I really begin to *see* them. A longshoreman does not act or speak like an accountant. Nor is an oceanographer like a computer programmer, a restaurateur, or a drummer in a rock band.

Usually, my characters' occupations come out of the background of the story. One historical novel I wrote, set in turn-of-the-century Sacramento, had a political background. In my mystery series, which revolves around a country-western bar on the San Francisco Peninsula, four of the characters own the bar and work there in various capacities.

You may have noticed that many of my plot ideas and characters come from life. I've used my passions and sorrows, my claustrophobia, my broken ribs, my interest in antiques. I shamelessly use the habits and hobbies and occupations of my family and friends—working in almost every interesting thing they do or say while I watch and listen. I've also used my dogs and cats and tropical fish, and my daughter's pet rabbit.

I make a practice of people-watching—discreetly, I hope—and make up one-liners that capture not only some aspect of their appearance, but also what I imagine their traits to be. For instance:

Only her eyes give her away—such sad, lost eyes, too big for her small face.

Dave was a Sagittarian, born old, dark eyes full of memories from the day he was born, but hope there too, always hope.

Eventually, I use all of these one-liners.

Drawing characters from life does not mean transferring real people into fiction *exactly* as you saw them. That method doesn't work, and it can get you into legal difficulties. I want every main character and some of the minor characters to be people the reader hasn't met before. So I use *parts* of real people—a gesture here, a mannerism there, a certain kind of jawline, a personality trait that seems intriguing—and put them together to make someone new and interesting.

Some years ago, I met a young man with a very attractive smile that would start far back behind his blue eyes, gradually move forward, and then brim over so that his eyes seemed filled with light. I have long since forgotten this man's name, but several of my characters, both male and female, have inherited versions of that smile.

Sometimes I'll come across models in catalogues or in magazines who bear a resemblance to the mental images I have of my characters. I put their pictures in my box. I keep my characters in mind while I'm performing other tasks and hold silent conversations with them. Gradually, they grow and take their places in the story. By the time I begin writing the novel, I know them so well I can hear what they would say, and see how they would react to various situations. They become real to me. They *must* become real to me, or they will never become real to my readers.

I like slightly eccentric characters. In one of my novels I developed a secondary character, the hero's sixty-something Uncle Simon, nicknamed Sly. Sly hadn't had a real home for many years. He traveled the United States, stopping off with one of his many cousins or nieces or nephews for a couple of months or so at a time. Invariably, he landed in trouble. Though he was immensely likable, he was also an inveterate gambler and womanizer.

But you can't just make up eccentric characters and drop them into the novel. They have to have a definite part to play that relates to the storyline. In *When the Spirit Is Willing,* Sly is being followed by a mysterious black car, a mini-mystery that eventually involves the heroine *and* the hero, with whom Sly is staying "temporarily."

When it looks as if the hero is falling in love with the heroine, Sly creates some mischief between them, because he's afraid if they get married his nephew won't want him around any more. In the same novel there is an eccentric Victorian ghost named Priscilla who materializes frequently and involves herself in everybody's business.

In *Shadow of a Doubt,* when Jamie is looking for something in her large handbag, instead of pawing through it, she upends it onto the nearest table. In this way, the reader sees exactly how much stuff she has in there and why the bag is as heavy as it is. This is a small, endearing character detail that the hero finds amusing. It acquires importance later on when Jamie incapacitates one of the bad guys by hitting him in a vulnerable area with her hefty handbag.

Conflict is the lifeblood of any novel, so you need to give it a lot of thought while you are plotting. Most conflict will fit into one of these categories: man or woman against nature; man or woman against himself or herself; man or woman against each other or against other people. In a romance novel, the main conflict (though not the only one) usually stems from something that is keeping two people apart emotionally. In a mystery, there is conflict that leads to the murder, conflict between the detective and the suspects, and so on. In science fiction, you might have conflicts between characters or ideologies, conflicts between worlds, conflicts between man or woman and machine.

What causes conflict? Jealousy, lust, pride, greed, resentment, insensitivity, adultery . . . the list goes on. Make your own list. Study each word, think about it in connection with your characters, and you are sure to come up with major and minor conflicts you can use in your novel.

Whenever anyone does anything in a novel, the writer should know *why*. Motivation—the inner drive, impulse, intention that causes a person to do something or act in a certain way—must always be taken into account. In real life, people often *seem* to perform random acts for no reason; in fiction you *must* reveal their motivation. To me, the *why* in a novel is a vital element of plotting. *What if* doesn't help me a whole lot, but *why* always activates my little gray cells.

Why is this woman doing that? *Why* is this man provoking that other woman? Why doesn't she run? Why is he so secretive? Why, why, why? Answering these questions sets your characters and your plot in motion.

Why did Mary kill John?

Because he had an affair with Laura.

Because he tried to kill Mary.

Because he stole her life savings.

Because he molested her child.

Because he molested her.

Because . . .

Different answers = different motivations, different characters, different stories.

Anything can be made believable if it is shown to be properly motivated; anything that is not motivated is difficult for your readers to believe.

Every novel needs suspense. Why else would the reader turn the page? Create anticipation and anxiety on your reader's part. Keep suspense in mind at all times while you are plotting your novel and developing your characters and when you are working on your synopsis.

One of the best ways to create suspense in your novel is to have at least one main character the reader will root for all the way through. Most readers won't identify with characters who are too perfect. The heroine of a romance novel doesn't have to be astonishingly beautiful. (I especially dislike a heroine who has an "exquisite profile.") Your readers will identify more readily if the heroine is just fairly attractive, but has a warm and wonderful smile.

The hero of a suspense novel doesn't have to be consistently macho, or too righteous or just too perfect. My heroes are often rogues, though endearing rogues.

Similarly, your villains don't have to be completely bad. The villain twirling his mustache in the "you-must-pay-the-rent" stereotype is not acceptable today. He can *be* thoroughly evil, but if he is, maybe he shouldn't *look* it. One recent serial killer was so cover-model handsome he had no problem attracting women so that he could kill them. Isn't that image more chilling than a villain with little beady eyes and an evil smile?

Give your heroes and heroines a few acceptable flaws and your villains a couple of believable virtues and your readers will identify and empathize and cheer and boo as they read.

Another way to make sure the reader will root for your main characters is to give them situations that are important to them. There was never any doubt in *Gone with the Wind* that Ashley was important to Scarlett; so was Tara, so was living through the war, so was never going hungry again. We could understand all of Scarlett's motivations—except, perhaps, why she couldn't see that Rhett Butler was worth ten of Ashley—so we rooted for her to get what she wanted.

Speaking of Rhett and Scarlett, this may be a good place to explain that I use the terms *hero* and *heroine* because I think they sound like people with real flesh and blood and distinctive personalities. I don't like the word *protagonist,* because it's not a word real people use. To me, it creates a distance between the writer and the character, the reader and the character. Though I use the term *main character,* I don't like it much either because it doesn't distinguish between male and female, good guy and bad guy. Also, I want my heroes and heroines to be slightly larger than life, with the emphasis on "slightly." We don't want Greek gods and goddesses here. On the other hand, if I make them too much like the people next door, they might be boring.

Readers want fiction to *seem* realistic and believable, even if it's invented. I have heard police officers complain that writers of mystery novels and movies never depict police procedure as it really is. Much of it, they say, is boring: filling out endless forms, waiting around courtrooms, asking countless people numerous questions. But who would read a novel or go to a movie in which the characters filled out endless forms, waited around courtrooms, or asked countless questions?

Keep all of this in mind as you work out your plot, but don't worry about it too much at this stage. You'll have plenty of time to check for suspense, believable motivation, and lively characters when you've finished your synopsis, or written your novel, or when you're revising it.

Here are a few more things to keep in mind as you work on your plot and characters:

1. Don't neglect the middle of your plot. Soon after I have some inklings about the beginning of my novel, I start thinking about the ending. The ending mustn't be too predictable, it mustn't be too easy, or too complicated. It mustn't go on too long. Above all, it must be believable.

Once I have the ending worked out, I have something to move the novel toward. In *Shadow of a Doubt,* for example, as soon as I knew Jamie was going to Bermuda to look into her friend Derry's death, and that Inspector Turner Garrett was going to help her—even though he'd been suspended from the police force on charges of brutality—I took time to figure out the ending.

By the time I had the end plotted, I knew much of what I needed for the middle.

By the middle of the novel the plot should develop, the characters should act and react. The law of cause and effect should govern what happens. Try not to think "and then what?" or "what next?" Instead, think "what would happen *because* of this?" and "what would be the direct result of *that?*" Consider this:

> *Because* Jamie does not believe her friend Derry's drowning was accidental, she goes to Bermuda to investigate. *Because* she is determined to investigate, she hooks up with Inspector Turner Garrett, who has just been suspended from the police force on suspicion of brutality. *Be-*

cause Turner has an agenda of his own, he agrees to help Jamie with her investigation . . .

2. While you are plotting the middle of your novel, think action. Is everyone sitting around in restaurants talking? An occasional lunch or dinner is O.K. if the dialogue is stimulating and has something to do with the story, but try not to have too many scenes take place at the dining table. As you move forward in your plotting and characterization, ask yourself every once in a while, "What is happening here?"

You don't want a novel filled with people's thoughts—not for a commercial novel, anyway. Include action scenes whenever you can. This doesn't mean you have to have car chases and fistfights all the time. But something should be *happening*. Even when your characters have to do some thinking, you can have them do it while they are working on something, or talking to one another. Don't let them just sit down and think. At least not for more than a few paragraphs.

In *When the Spirit Is Willing,* as the heroine is remodeling a Victorian house, I have her actually dismantling kitchen cabinets and putting up drywall while she's talking to other characters.

In another novel, *As Years Go By,* one of the characters is grooming a dog while a conversation is going on. *Brief* references to the grooming make the scene more visual and add interest. In the same novel, two characters discuss a situation while climbing up to King Arthur's Castle in Tintagel, Cornwall.

It's best to avoid having talking heads. Unusual settings and events going on in the background can add a great deal to a scene.

3. We have covered four of the five W's: *What* kind of novel? *Who* are the characters? *Where* is the story taking place? *Why* do the characters do the things they do?

The fifth W is *when*. *When* does your story take place? This year? Seventeenth century? The immediate future? The year 3000? During World War II?

You need to think about chronology the whole time you are working on your novel, during which it's very easy to forget how much time has passed. Errors can distract the reader. If you've had enough sentences beginning, "The next day . . ." or "A week later" or "When the daffodils bloomed" to add up to three months, but then one of the characters makes the statement that a month has passed since "it" happened, readers will quickly sense that something isn't quite right.

I keep a calendar for every novel, filling in the spaces as the plot grows. In this way, I never lose track of the chronology. The notes are brief: *Turner agrees to help Jamie look into Derry's death. Jamie questions Anna Campbell. Jamie and Turner are abducted from the boat.*

Buy a calendar with fairly large squares for each day of the month. (If you work on a computer, you can buy software that will generate a calen-

dar with the correct dates for any year you require, past or future.)

Whether you have used a box like mine to hold
your notes and other materials, or have written
everything down on colored pages or index cards,
or used computer files to hold all the elements of
your plot, you are now ready to start writing a
synopsis. Take a deep breath, flex your fingers,
and begin!

◄ 4 ►

The Synopsis, Your Selling Tool

Many novelists say that a synopsis is their most important selling tool. I believe that *good writing* is the writer's most important selling tool, but certainly a well-thought-out, well-constructed synopsis comes a close second.

In recent years, publishing houses have cut staffs and don't have the number of first readers they used to have—people who sat all day reading through what is called the "slush pile" or manuscripts that come in "over the transom," more professionally known as unsolicited manuscripts. Sending out a synopsis rather than an entire novel saves an editor time. It lets the editor know you have the ability to organize and plot a complete novel. If that kind of novel is not suitable for the particular publishing house, the editor will recognize that fact immediately and tell you so. On the other hand, if it does seem suitable and the synopsis is well written, the editor will often encourage the writer to complete the novel and submit it, thus turning an unsolicited manuscript into a solicited one.

Some editors want a short synopsis, six pages or so; others want a long one of twenty pages plus. It's probably a good idea to work out a ratio to the projected length of the book. I write twenty to thirty pages (double-spaced) for a 340-page, 85,000-word, finished novel manuscript.

Question: What exactly is a synopsis?

Answer: A summary of the story.

Sometimes publishers will offer a previously published author a contract on the basis of a novel *proposal,* which consists of a synopsis and sample chapters of the novel. (N.B. Check with the editor to see which chapters he wants. Typically, it's the first three, but some may want to see a variety of chapters.)

Many new writers are horrified at the very idea of writing a summary of a novel. It's not possible, they say, to condense a story of 60,000 to 100,000 words into six pages, or ten pages, or twenty. Actually, there is nothing easier than writing a good synopsis. So don't agonize over it—just do it!

Before writing your novel, you need to know what it's about. Even if editors didn't want to see a synopsis before considering a novel, you should write one, simply because it's the best possible guide to have on hand as you write your novel. A synopsis is your map, your chronology, your security blanket.

I cannot tell you precisely how to write your synopsis; I can only give you a couple of versions of how I write mine and hope you'll find one or both helpful.

The synopsis is traditionally written in present tense. Your name and address and telephone number should appear on the first page at the top left corner. Pages should be numbered and typed double-spaced. The title, or a key word from it if it's long, should appear at the top of every page along with your last name.

I don't even think of starting a synopsis until I have made all my notes on characters, plot, settings, occupations, conflicts, story situations, and so forth. By the time I begin the first rough synopsis, my notebook is pretty well filled and I have a fair idea of the storyline.

I always start writing the synopsis first thing in the morning, so that I can finish it in one day. I try to write at white heat, working straight through without referring to my notes, because by now everything is in my mind. I aim to write fast, without stopping to think, "How am I going to get these people out of this situation?" or "How will I fill this black hole?" or "This isn't going to work." I don't worry about typos or repetitions in this first draft. The idea is to get the storyline down. Anything you write down can be improved upon later.

One editor I've worked with gives this advice on writing the synopsis: "I want the writer to focus on main characters and show others just passing through. Otherwise, my attention can be jarred from the primary story. I don't expect fantastic prose or witty dialogue (in a synopsis). I'm looking for the basic facts, how the story begins and how it ends. Atmosphere is not the key factor at this point. Clarity and conciseness are much more important. If the basic story works, *then* I read the book to see if the writing holds up and to see how the characters are developed. Synopses are primarily sources of information.

"My advice to writers worried over the readability of their synopsis is to give it to a friend, and see if he can follow it. If, after reading it, the friend is able to relate to the author the story's highlights and keep all the characters straight, chances are this is going to work for an editor as well."

After I have written this first rough synopsis, often running to fifty or sixty pages of sprawling story, I read through all my notes again to make sure I haven't left anything out. All that I know about the story should be in this rough draft. I mark appropriate spots where chapter endings might come—places in the story where something is about to happen—so that if I cut to a new chapter at that point, the reader will feel compelled to read on. I don't like the common term *cliffhangers,* because some writers take it too literally and make up all kinds of sensational chapter endings that have little to do with the story. Just bear in mind that the end of a chapter is an easy place for readers to put a novel down, and you don't want them to do that!

With this rough draft in hand, I look at each

chapter division and ask myself questions such as, "Where is the conflict in this chapter? Is there enough action? Enough suspense? Whose viewpoint are we in?" If necessary, I make changes so that I can answer these questions and others that may come up as I read. Then I save this copy for reference.

On a separate copy of the synopsis, I start cutting and editing, revising and polishing, until I have twenty to thirty fairly tight pages that include only what the editor absolutely must know in order to evaluate this novel. This is the *editor's synopsis,* and it's the one I send along when I submit the first three chapters. Both synopses— rough and revised—are subject to change as I actually *write* the first three chapters of the novel.

The final synopsis of my romantic suspense novel *Shadow of a Doubt* began like this:

> Two armed men, with stockings over their faces, gloves on their hands, enter the Tudor Tavern, a popular and crowded bar in Bermuda, and proceed to shoot at random, creating general pandemonium and killing two of the patrons before they leave as suddenly as they arrived.
>
> The action then cuts to Jamie Maxwell, age 27, tall, nicely put together, not a beauty, but attractive, with a mane of red hair that looks as if it had been curled with a hot corkscrew.
>
> Jamie is a meeting planner for a major software company in Boston, and she has come to Bermuda to consult with the police department. Recently, her best friend and colleague, Derry Riley, had visited Bermuda, planning on a two-week vacation. On a trip on a glass-bottomed boat, Derry had fallen overboard from the fantail and drowned.

At least, that's what the police report says.

On May 10, having made inquiries at Hamilton Police Station, Jamie is referred to Turner Garrett, an English Bermudian—age 35, tall, lean, athletically built, dark-haired, dark-eyed. Turner is an Inspector with Bermuda's somewhat secretive Special Services Squad, located in an anonymous-looking building in the small community of Walbridge, on Bermuda's incredibly beautiful south shore.

The synopsis goes on from there, adding more details of the main characters' traits along the way: Jamie is untidy and outgoing; Turner is private and almost obsessively neat. I *briefly* describe other characters and settings as they appear in the storyline. Note the emphasis on *briefly*.

I like to include some dialogue occasionally, to bring the characters to life and make reading more interesting. For instance:

Jamie is questioning Lathrop, a possible witness to her friend's death; he tells her the only person on deck was Bobbie Kenyon, a crew member who had turned up for work stoned a couple of times and had finally "done a bunk."

"After the accident?" Jamie asks.

Lathrop frowns, then says, "You think it might be connected? You think maybe somebody did the bloke in?"

"What do you think?" she counters.

As you can see, I write the synopsis very simply, as if I am telling someone the story. I write down the whole plot, including the ending. *Especially the ending,* as for *Shadow of a Doubt*:

In the cabin, Turner flings the contents of the whiskey bottle in the face of one of the men and Jamie flails her shoulder bag and incapacitates the other. After retrieving the guards' guns, she and Turner take cover in a locker that holds life preservers. When one of the guards finds them and attacks Turner, Jamie hits him with one of the life preservers, which bursts open, showering them all with white powder—cocaine.

Turner forces Connor Hollingsworth at gunpoint to take the boat back to Hamilton where Connor is arrested.

The next day, Turner declares his love for Jamie and asks her to marry him. She accepts his proposal.

You must *always* let the editor know how the story turns out—not, of course, simply, *everybody lives happily ever after,* or *John kills Mary,* but precisely *how* the main characters are going to go about resolving their difficulties—in summary form. I've read a lot of synopses by beginning writers that leave the ending vague. This is not a good idea; if the editor doesn't know how you intend to finish the story, he or she cannot judge whether the story will be successful or not and will therefore be much less inclined to tell you to go ahead with the novel.

Sometimes, I confess, I have trouble getting the storyline worked out. I can sense where the story is going, and I have written all my notes on plot and character, but the entire story refuses to come clear in my mind. That's when I use my second method of writing a synopsis, which makes some writers laugh. But it works for me and I'm in favor of anything that works.

What I do is this: After I have all my notes

ready, I put them into the computer just as they are. Here's an example for my mystery series:

> Crew in overalls comes to dig body up. Charlie awakened. She is mad at Zack for calling the media. After they'd discovered the corpse he'd lectured them all solemnly on the necessity of keeping their discovery a secret.

> Charlie's father was Greek. Charlie eats Greek food occasionally but mother was overweight so she's wary of it.

> Following an earthquake you should put power plugs on major appliances to prevent damage from a power surge when electricity is restored.

Then I read each paragraph carefully, indicating in the margin whether it seems to belong in the beginning, the middle, or the end. With the computer, I can then start shifting blocks of text to their proper places. If you use a typewriter or pen and legal pad, you can cut and paste or retype.

With every section in its proper place, I begin to see the storyline more clearly and add transitions and extra paragraphs as needed. Once the storyline comes through clearly, I save this copy and do my cutting and polishing on another copy for the editor.

I think of these two methods as *different* forms of sculpture. When sculptors work with clay, they start out with an armature, then add clay to it, shaping it until it becomes the desired object. When working with stone, they start with a big piece of rock and chip away at it until the essential object is revealed.

Even though I've done all this work on a synopsis, I do not stick slavishly to it as I write the novel. I make changes, moving blithely ahead and writing my story the way that seems best at that point. No editor has ever said to me, "Why did you make this story different from the synopsis?" Sometimes the change is slight, or I may introduce a new character and a subplot that wasn't in the original synopsis. Or I may change characters' names and the color of their hair or eyes. However, I make only those changes that I think are improvements on the original. If I want to make major changes and the book is already under contract, I check with my editor first. Other than that, the entire novel is subject to change by me until the final copy actually leaves my desk.

I hope you will develop a positive attitude toward synopsis writing. I readily admit I used to hate writing a synopsis. I'd rather write the whole novel, I would say. Well, I'm a hard-headed Englishwoman, and if I can change my attitudes, anyone can.

◄ 5 ►

The Why and Who of Point of View

I am a purist—well, let's be honest, I've been called a fanatic—on the subject of point of view. Some otherwise good stories and novels have, in my opinion, been ruined by writers who did not understand point of view.

A reminder here: Nothing I say should be taken as gospel. In this chapter I may advise you against doing things that you will see many wonderful, well-established writers doing. All I can do is tell you the advantages and pitfalls I have perceived in the various ways of using viewpoint. Once you fully understand all the rules, feel free to break them. But if you do break them, know *why*.

There are several ways of treating viewpoint in fiction. You can write in the second-person viewpoint, addressing the reader directly. *You are walking along, singing a song, when suddenly you see* . . . This method is very awkward and is not recommended for fiction, unless you are writing humor.

You can write as the author, from the outside, watching what everyone is doing, knowing what everyone is thinking. Fiction writers used to do this quite openly, with *dear reader,* or *gentle reader.* Unless it's done humorously, this method would not be acceptable to today's readers.

You can still use this omniscient viewpoint, in which you, the author, view your characters from the outside, and at the same time reveal each character's thoughts and feelings. Nowadays, however, the omniscient viewpoint is used with a little more subtlety, so that the reader is not aware of the writer behind the scenes.

You might decide to write from the viewpoint of a minor character who watches and/or participates in the action of the main characters. This method tends to distance the reader from the story, so I wouldn't recommend it for any but short passages, unless your novel is a reminiscence, like John Van Druten's play, *I Remember Mama.*

Let's consider viewpoints that are most commonly used in fiction today, viewpoints that involve the reader on an emotional level. You may write in first person from the point of view of the main character, as though you *are* the main character. Traditionally used in romantic gothic novels, the first-person viewpoint is still often used today in mainstream novels, romantic suspense, and in mysteries, especially in series, when the main character has an established, distinctive voice. To quote from Marcia Muller's *Till the Butchers Cut Him Down:*

> I made the best decision of my life on a high meadow in California's White Mountains, where I'd gone to watch for the wild mustangs.
> . . .Decision time, I thought. Middle-of-your-life-cross-roads, important stuff. Make the right choice and it's golden; make the wrong one—
> I didn't want to think about that.

Alternatively, you can write in third-person viewpoint. As with first-person viewpoint, in third-person point of view, the writer *becomes* the viewpoint character and *sees, hears, touches, wants,* and *remembers* only what that character sees, hears, touches, wants, and remembers. The only information readers are given is the information the viewpoint character has (except for things that can be demonstrated in dialogue or body language or innuendo).

Now, to confuse matters even more, third-person viewpoint can be approached in more than one way: In one, the writer writes only through the viewpoint of the main character—a very limited choice. This third-person, limited viewpoint used to be the only one that was acceptable in romance novels, and traditionally it was the heroine's viewpoint. Many romance editors today want the hero's viewpoint to be included as well.

The viewpoint I'm going to examine most extensively is not only the most popular (in novel-writing), it is the most likely to give the writer problems. This is the third-person, multiple viewpoint, in which the author writes from the point of view of more than one character. This is my favorite method: I've used it in romances and novels of intrigue, and in a couple of mainstream novels.

No matter whose point of view you use at a given place in your novel, you must *become* that person. Obviously, the mind of a teenager will not be like that of a forty-year-old male or a thirty-year-old female or a sixty-year-old female, or even that of a teenager from another country, or another era. Like an actor, you must take on the characteristics of each of the characters through whose viewpoint you are writing and presenting the story to your readers. Your characters should not think, act, react, or talk like you.

Most of my writing is done from the viewpoint of a male or female between twenty-five and thirty-five years of age (though I am not in that age group), so when my twenty-five-year-old character turns on the radio, she listens to the top forty, and talks, thinks, dresses, and dances like a contemporary young woman.

For instance, in *When the Spirit Is Willing,* I used the viewpoint of the heroine, Laura, the hero, Carter, the heroine's daughter Jessica, and the hero's Uncle Simon, known as Sly. The other major character in this book is Priscilla, a ghost. I did not use her viewpoint because I felt it would be too much of a wrench for the reader to try to see the action through the eyes and senses of a ghost.

My test for deciding to switch point of view is whether or not the switch will add to the reader's understanding and enjoyment of the story. (I do not, however, worry about this while I'm writing the first draft.)

Here are a few passages from *When the Spirit Is Willing,* using a different person's viewpoint each time:

Viewpoint 1. Laura, the heroine, third-person viewpoint:

> She picked up her flashlight, then hesitated. There it was again—that odd, spine-tingling sensation that made her feel as if someone was watching her. She'd felt it several times a day since she'd moved into the house on Humboldt Street. Sometimes there were other weird sensations—a whisper of air on the staircase, a movement caught out of the corner of her eye, a patch of heat or cold in an otherwise temperate room.

Because I used such phrases as "made her feel," "she'd felt it," "movement caught out of the corner of her eye," the reader is kept quite firmly inside Laura throughout this entire passage.

If I had written *Laura picked up her flashlight, a frown on her pretty face,* I would have slipped out of Laura's viewpoint by looking at her from the outside. Either I'm in someone else's viewpoint and that person is watching Laura, or I'm omniscient. I cannot see my own face without a mirror, so how could Laura see hers without a mirror?

I stress this because I so frequently see manuscripts in which an author puts the reader inside a character's viewpoint, then writes: *Feeling vaguely frightened, Clare tried to relax in her seat, a worried expression spoiling the delicate beauty of her face.*

Not only has the author *leaped* out of Clare's viewpoint, but Clare now seems pretty conceited. If you want to be sure you haven't slipped out of viewpoint, you might try mentally casting a particular section into first person. You would not write, *I tried to relax in my seat, a worried expression spoiling the delicate beauty of my face,* unless you have a lot more confidence than I have!

Since I see published novels in which writers seem unable to hold to one viewpoint, some writers and editors obviously disagree with me. But I think it's jarring to let readers inside a character and then show that character from the outside.

There are many ways to describe your viewpoint character without shifting viewpoint or resorting to the trite method of having a character look at herself in a mirror. I usually wait until I shift the story into another character's point of view, and then I let the second character do the describing. Or I might have another character say something to the viewpoint character that reveals what she looks like: "That green dress really matches your eyes." "You look like an ad for sunshine and vitamins."

Viewpoint 2. Jessica, the heroine's daughter, third-person viewpoint:

> Jessica slammed her bedroom door. She was getting sick of her mom yelling at her for something that wasn't

her fault. "You got me in trouble again, Priscilla," she grumbled, throwing herself down on the bed.

She heard the creak of the rocking chair. "I'm sorry, Jessica," Priscilla said.

The sentence, "Jessica slammed her bedroom door," could be in anyone's viewpoint. However, "She was getting sick of her mom yelling at her for something that wasn't her fault," or, "She heard the creak of the rocking chair," can be only in Jessica's viewpoint, because Jessica's senses are involved.

Viewpoint 3. Here's Carter's viewpoint, again in third person. Carter is a museum curator, and he talks (and thinks) in a rather formal manner:

It was like watching a Polaroid picture come to life, Carter thought with awe. A twentieth-century marvel, which, in this instance, had a nineteenth-century result. The woman who had slowly materialized in the Boston rocker was definitely of the nineteenth century. She was corseted and bustled, richly dressed in jade green, her small feet tightly encased in black buttoned boots, her face innocent of makeup, her long curly brown hair drawn softly back into a bun under a hat trimmed with fluffy feathers.

She was smiling at him, her green eyes gleaming. Distantly, he heard Laura exclaim hoarsely in disbelief, but over that he heard the other woman's voice. "Hello there, Carter, you're looking more like yourself today."

He remembered that voice. Mischievous, lilting, it had filled his early childhood with laughter . . . and love.

Priscilla.

The reason I quote that fairly long passage is to show what would happen if I *didn't* stay in Carter's viewpoint throughout that scene:

> It was like watching a Polaroid picture come to life, Carter thought with awe. A twentieth-century marvel, which, in this instance, had a nineteenth-century result.
> Laura couldn't believe the evidence of her own eyes. The woman who had slowly materialized in the Boston rocker was corseted and bustled, richly dressed in jade green, her small feet tightly encased in black buttoned boots, her face innocent of makeup, her long curly brown hair drawn softly back into a bun under a hat trimmed with fluffy feathers.
> Priscilla smiled at Carter, her green eyes gleaming. She thought he looked more like his old self today. "Hello there, Carter," she said to him.
> Carter remembered that voice.

Pretty bad! When you are writing in one person's viewpoint, you should *stay* in that person's viewpoint, at least for a while. There is nothing more distressing to readers than having a novel hop from the mind of one character to another. This example may seem exaggerated, but I have seen much worse—manuscripts in which the writer entered the mind of almost everyone in a restaurant, including the waiters and the cook back in his kitchen!

How long should you stay in someone's viewpoint? Usually for the length of a scene or a chapter. It is certainly easier to switch viewpoints smoothly when you do it at the end of a scene or chapter. For instance:

Laura couldn't think why she loathed the thought of Carter Kincaid buying her house and living in it when she was gone. For a minute there, when he'd made his announcement, she had wanted to punch him right on his perfectly shaped nose.

End of chapter.
Beginning of next chapter:

"O.K. Sly, let's talk," Carter said firmly as he drove toward his apartment.

An easy switch from Laura to Carter and also an easy transition to a new chapter.

Changing viewpoint at the end of a scene would be similar, but this often requires an extra space or two to make sure the shift is clear to the readers.

Laura had the horrible feeling it was her fault Priscilla had decided to make herself scarce. She and Carter should have left well enough alone. It seemed to her there was a strong possibility that Priscilla would never show herself again.

(Extra Space)

"How do I go about tracing the former owners of a house?" Carter asked Mildred Whittock on Monday morning.

I have successfully changed viewpoint and scene here. You'll notice this is done abruptly. It works best if you don't shilly-shally by having someone walk out of the room, have a night's sleep, get up the next morning, and then go on with the story.

Now let's break the rules and shift viewpoint from one character to another right in the middle of a scene. We have been in Laura's viewpoint for some time. Then:

> She wished she could talk to Carter Kincaid privately. Maybe he'd have some idea of what she could do to get Priscilla to move somewhere else. She had no intention of sharing her home with a ghost, especially such a mischievous ghost.
>
> "Perhaps we could go out to dinner," Carter said as if he'd read her mind.
>
> Laura was startled, which was hardly surprising under the circumstances. Carter gazed meaningfully at her, trying to communicate with a couple of quick sidelong glances at Priscilla that he thought they should discuss this peculiar situation in private. To himself, he also admitted to another motive. He'd liked holding Laura in his arms. He wanted to do it again. His always-creative mind was already painting a seduction scenario—a long romantic dinner, candlelight, soft music, wine. At some point in the evening, he would take her into his arms again. . .
>
> "How about lunch," Laura suggested.

The sentence—*Laura was startled, which was hardly surprising under the circumstances*—begins the shift of viewpoint away from Laura. The next sentence—*Carter gazed meaningfully at her, trying to communicate . . .*—completes the shift into Carter's viewpoint.

The reason I changed viewpoint in the middle

of that scene was to show how Carter had reacted to the previous scene, which was in Laura's viewpoint and involved Carter's taking Laura in his arms. In this way, I could add to the sexual tension. The reader knows now that Carter wants Laura. The last sentence sets up some conflict. Laura is not going along with Carter's romantic ideas.

It is all right to change viewpoint almost anywhere, *if* there is a good reason for doing so, *if* the transition is made completely clear to the reader, and *if* the writer knows *exactly* why she or he is making the change. Otherwise it's best not to shift viewpoint until the next scene or chapter.

A couple of things to watch for: Suppose your viewpoint character is recalling something from the past, and you decide to write the scene in flashback. In other words, you want to take the reader back to that scene and *show* it, rather than have the viewpoint character *tell* another character about it. Even though the scene is being shown to the reader, it is being shown through the recollections of the viewpoint character. You should not slip into someone else's viewpoint in a flashback scene.

Suppose you are writing a novel that deals with reincarnation. Under hypnosis, the hero is reliving his previous life. Clearly, during this scene, the writer cannot move into someone else's thoughts, because the hero cannot read minds!

I'm also against changing viewpoint while the characters are having a telephone conversation.

Suppose you are writing in John's viewpoint, and John calls Mary on the telephone. While he talks to her, all of a sudden you tell the reader what Mary is thinking. This would make readers feel as if they've been pulled bodily through the telephone line!

Occasionally, the viewpoint character in a novel is the villain, but more often, determining which character will tell your story shows readers whom you want them to root for. For this reason, in certain kinds of novels, it's best to stay only in the main character's point of view. Not only does the writer in effect become the main character, but the *reader* becomes the main character as well. In a story about a woman in jeopardy, if the author keeps in mind at all times that the *woman* is the viewpoint character, that this is *her* story, the reader feels her fear, her anger, her helplessness; recognizes her courage; and roots for her to make it safely through to the end and achieve her goal.

A good question to ask yourself when you are plotting is, whose story is this? Which character will the reader care about most? Who has the most to lose or win? Who is going to have the most internal conflict because of this? Whoever that character is should be the viewpoint character for the major part of the novel.

I often use the point of view of secondary characters as well as of main characters, but I do so *sparingly* and only when it will enhance the story's effect. For example, in *When the Spirit Is Willing,* I wanted to hint that Priscilla was a ghost *before* she revealed herself as such to main characters Laura and Carter. To do this, I showed Priscilla through the viewpoint of Laura's daughter Jessica, the only character who knew from the beginning that Priscilla was in the house.

I also occasionally used the viewpoint of Carter's Uncle Sly, to let the reader know why he was trying to come between Carter and Laura. I wanted the reader to like him, so his actions had to be explained.

Sometimes for a scene in which none of the main characters is present, you can use a minor character's viewpoint to good effect. I often do this to add suspense. The reader knows there is a threat, perhaps, before the main character knows.

Here's how it worked in my novel, *Shadow of a Doubt*. The scene is written in the viewpoint of a man named Kyle, whom the readers have not met before the beginning of this scene, but whom they know by now was involved in a recent shooting:

> "Find him," the chief said. "Get the film."
> When the chief got that snotty tone in his voice there was no arguing with him. "Yes sir," Kyle and his partner said in unison. "What if he has it on him?" Kyle asked. "What if he catches us getting it?"
> Another sigh. The chief leaned back. The meeting was over. "We use our own discretion, right?" Kyle suggested.
> There was no answer. Do what you have to do, Kyle interpreted.

Using Kyle's viewpoint here adds suspense and shows a threat. In this novel, I used the hero's viewpoint, the heroine's, Kyle's, and an occasional omniscient viewpoint for dramatic effect. I did not go into the villain's viewpoint because I didn't want the reader to know who the villain was. If you go into a villain's viewpoint under these circumstances, you have to resort to all kinds of trickery so readers won't guess that he is the villain. I don't like to trick the reader.

Let's take a quick look at omniscient viewpoint, in which the writer, rather than a viewpoint character, is looking at the scene and describing it to the reader. I often *set* a scene this way, before moving into a character's viewpoint. I did so in the beginning of my novel, *The Wainwright Secret*.

> The body lay face down in the shallow river. Minnows, darting between the reeds like quicksilver, played hide and seek among floating strands of the intruder's blond hair, brushing against his well-manicured fingers and the excellent fabric of his tailored suit. The mist over the water was thick now, sometimes billowing in the slight breeze, making the body appear to be moving. But it wasn't moving. It would never move again.

In omniscient viewpoint, it is possible to enter the thoughts of one or more characters while also looking at them from the outside. In *Shadow of a Doubt* I moved into and out of one character's viewpoint in a single paragraph to make the suspense more subjective:

> A young black waitress, carrying a tray loaded with beer glasses, was the first to see the two men enter the

lounge. Both wore trench coats. Both had semiopaque stockings over their heads. The waitress stared blankly at them, thinking how strange they looked, their features flat and unrecognizable, their hair invisible, their ears making odd-shaped bumps at the sides of their heads. Then she saw the guns pointing at her—matte black guns, handguns, two to each man.

The crash of the loaded tray falling to the floor brought every head around. A ripple of paralyzing fear ran through the room as the patrons' eyes followed the woman's fixed gaze.

When overused, omniscient viewpoint can be annoying because the reader begins to wonder just who is saying all this, but used sparingly, it can be effective and can enhance the story.

It's impossible to make rigid rules about which viewpoint to use, and when and how often you should change it, if at all. The only advice I can give you with any authority is to study the various approaches to viewpoint carefully, so that you will always know which one you are using and why.

◄ 6 ►

Developing Your
Own Voice

I would like you to think about something that is often neglected by new writers: style. Or as I prefer to call it, writing with your own voice.

A word of caution here: Developing your own voice does not mean that you can ignore the basic techniques of novel writing. It does mean that you can, and should, put your own stamp on those techniques.

I delayed beginning to write because I was sure I didn't know anything that would be useful in fiction writing. Eventually, of course, I realized that I do have quite a lot of knowledge and experience. I have seen death. I have seen a baby born. I have loved someone who didn't love me. I have loved someone who *did* love me. I have known jealousy and greed and hope and hatred and envy, pain and joy and shame. All of this became part of my writing style, my voice.

As a child, I read mostly English classics—Thackeray, Dickens, Austen. I also read the kind of books that had to be kept secret from parental eyes, usually in my bed under the blankets by flashlight. I read constantly, avidly, indiscriminately, but when I finally got around to writing myself, I did not draw deliberately or consciously on any of these reading experiences. Every once in a while, I come upon advice to beginning writers that suggests that they should read their favorite author and try to imitate that style until they develop a style of their own.

This advice appalls me. In my opinion, the only way you can develop your own voice is to live your life as fully as possible and spend a great deal of time listening to what is going on in your head. Everything you have seen and done and smelled and touched and listened to and experienced has gone into making you the person you are. And if you want your writing to be original and authentic, it is *your* voice that should come through.

Years ago, I read Eric Berne's handbook of transactional analysis, *The Games People Play*. There's a story in there about a little boy who:

> . . . sees and hears birds with delight. Then the "good father" comes along and feels he should "share" the experience and help his son "develop." He says: "That's a jay, and this is a sparrow." The moment the little boy is concerned with which is a jay and which is a sparrow, he can no longer see the birds or hear them sing. *He has to see and hear them the way his father wants him to.* [The emphasis is mine.]

The first time I read this story, I pondered over it for a long time. It had touched a chord inside me, but it took me a while to realize why: It freed me from listening to other people's voices! I had certain opinions, as most of us do, opinions about life, politics, sex, relationships. But when I started listening to my own voice I realized these opinions were not really my own. They were either opinions I had copied from others, or opinions I had developed in opposition to others. I began asking myself, *Is this really what I think? Does this seem true to me?* All of this questioning became part of my writing voice.

I enjoy visiting art galleries. At first glance, the paintings I like are all very different from one another, but a more careful study shows that they have something in common—none of them is representational. I don't care for painted images that could have been taken with a camera. I want art in which the artist shows me a new way of looking at things—his or her way, a way that I would not have seen without his or her help.

Helping the reader see things through *your* eyes, *your* thoughts, *your* attitudes, is part of writing with your own voice.

When I decide on a background for one of my novels, I check the accuracy of everything I want to write about. And this search for authenticity is part of my voice.

I love to travel. I love to meet people, especially unusual people. Parts of them and parts of the places I visit go into my novels, and my voice is there showing the reader, *through my characters,* how I feel about those people and those places.

Using this approach, your work will be unique and original because no one else will have exactly your reactions.

I draw heavily on my own experiences, as I'm sure most writers do. Read my books and you will know me. The food the characters eat is food I have enjoyed or hated. The wines, the emotions, the flowers, the allergies are all mine.

Of course, I have written of murder without murdering anyone. But I have had murderous thoughts on occasion. Who among us has not? I have also had experiences that made my heart race with fear. I can draw on the emotions and the physical reactions I had to those experiences, even if I don't use the actual experiences. (Mostly they were too tame to scare anybody but me.)

Most real experiences can't be used in fiction exactly as they happened. Viewed through your characters' eyes, instead of your own, those experiences must change. Often I have read a passage in a beginning writer's manuscript and have commented that it's not too believable, only to have the writer tell me, "But you said to write from my own experience and that's how it really happened."

Yes, by all means, use your experiences *if they lend themselves to the stories you're writing,* but allow them to change, to evolve, to entertain, according to the needs of your story and its particular *fictional* reality. Use them as jumping-off points.

Some writers insist you should be able to sum

up your novel's meaning in one sentence. I'm not sure that's always possible, but it's a good idea to keep track of what you are trying to say through your novel as a whole and to make sure what you've written makes the point you want to make.

Reading the manuscript of a children's book recently, I had to point out to the author that the story as a whole was saying that if you played hooky from school, you could get all kinds of rewards. Obviously, this was not the message the writer had in mind!

In my various writings I have addressed the themes of what we are doing to our oceans; the often rocky relationship between parents and children; how to deal with grief and misplaced guilt, among others. The central ideas I want to convey in my novels are those about which I feel strongly. Your issues will undoubtedly be different. They should be. If those issues will illustrate the themes of your novels, use them to reflect your own voice.

None of this means that you, the writer, *or* your characters should get up on a soapbox and preach about favorite causes. Instead, let your characters' *actions* illustrate your themes.

Finding your own voice is not easy. Beginning writers often talk to me about their lives in a manner that is witty and articulate and intelligent. And then what happens? Many bright people think that the only good writing is "highbrow" writing, and the minute they start writing dialogue on a keyboard, their writing becomes stilted and stiff and clichéd. Their characters move with all the vitality of Lot's wife, *after* she turned around for that last look. These same characters *interject, interpolate, harangue* or *declaim.* They never just *say* something; they *expound* or *interject,* and use words like *opprobrium* or *recalcitrant.* Good writing is clear writing, writing that *communicates.*

When I first arrived in the United States from England, I made a grocery list for my husband to take to the Air Force base commissary. He was soon home again, without several items. He'd had no idea that a joint was meat for roasting. He didn't know serviettes were paper napkins, jelly meant gelatin, not jam, treacle was molasses, or that when I asked for a packet of biscuits I didn't want *biscuits,* I wanted cookies. Obviously, I had to learn to communicate with words that meant something to *him.*

This is the whole idea behind any kind of writing, whether it's the great American novel, a letter to the editor, or a memo to the boss. The person on the receiving end—your reader—has to be able to understand what you mean to say.

While developing your own style, then, remember that the best writing is not purple or flowery prose or writing that is meant to impress the reader with your esoteric knowledge. Simple writing, clear writing, straightforward writing, can be beautiful enough to move a reader to tears.

In 1859, this is how Charles Dickens began *A Tale of Two Cities:*

It was the best of times, it was the worst of times, it
was the age of wisdom, it was the age of foolishness, it
was the epoch of belief, it was the epoch of incredulity, it
was the season of Light, it was the season of Darkness, it
was the spring of hope, it was the winter of despair . . .

The passage is as easy to read and understand
today as it was when Dickens wrote it. I wonder
though if it was easy to write. Perhaps for Dickens
it was easy; for me, writing is never easy. The
easier it reads, the freer it sounds, the more I've
had to prod and poke at my brain to produce the
words.

Hemingway said:

The first and most important thing for writers today is
to strip language clean, to lay it bare down to the bone.

I don't always get my prose pared down to the
bone, though it's something to aim for. I do try to
eliminate the fat, the extra words, the words that
are not necessary to tell the story. Writers are
always being advised to use adjectives sparingly,
but I'm rather fond of them. I think prose loses a
lot of its color if you don't use them. "A *bony*
woman with a *flat* nose" gives me a more vivid
picture than "a woman." Ditto, "a *portly* man
wearing a *tweed* cap." All the same, I *try* to avoid
using more than one or two adjectives at a time,
and I cut them out when I'm absolutely sure they
aren't serving a legitimate purpose.

I have to watch out for adverbs, too, because I
tend to sprinkle them liberally after "said" in my

first draft: "He said softly." "She said lovingly." I know all the arguments against this. "He whispered" and "she murmured" are stronger. But sometimes "He said softly" *sounds* right.

Moderation is the key word.

I do follow most of the rules of English grammar, with some exceptions during dialogue sequences, when they are appropriate to the characters speaking. Most people don't use proper grammar in conversation, especially if they get excited. But when you are writing narrative sequences or transitions, the grammar should be as good as you can make it.

This goes for spelling, too. Computer spelling checkers are not infallible—they don't notice if you type *too* instead of *to,* or *stare* instead of *stair* or *their* instead of *there.* Since these are all real words, the spelling checker accepts them as correct, even if they are wrong in a particular context. So be sure to proofread your manuscript for errors!

Try to write *visually,* remembering to use strong specific nouns—"the brownstone" or "the bungalow" rather than "the house." Use active rather than passive verbs, verbs that help to paint a picture: "He *strode* across the empty lobby," or "She *jogged* along the boardwalk," or "The German shepherd *darted* between parked cars and into traffic."

Strong active verbs can do wonders for your style: "Claire *attacked* her oysters." "Sailboats *scudded* across the Sound." "Dan *scuffed* sand with his bare toes."

Part II
THE WRITING

◀ 7 ▶

Getting Off to
a Good Start

When I first tried to write fiction, I used to get frustrated listening to experienced writers talk about characterization, plot, dialogue, viewpoint, work habits, etc. I kept wanting to say, "Yes, that's all very well, and I need to learn it, but how should I actually *write?* When I put my fingers to my keyboard, how do I make my ideas come out?"

I realize now why none of the speakers covered this subject. It's almost impossible to describe the actual writing process. But I'm going to try.

Before writing a particular chapter, read the corresponding section of your synopsis, sit back for a while and try to imagine the scene in your mind. Then begin to write.

Don't agonize over every word or sentence trying to get it right, and don't worry about going too slowly or too quickly. Just do it. Stay focused on this particular part of your story and on nothing else. Let your brain guide your fingers. Write words down as they come to you, striving for that altered state of consciousness in which you can listen to and see the story as it unfolds in your mind's eye.

One best-selling novelist has said the experience is like being an invisible participant in the scene, seeing your characters without their seeing you. Another author feels that she has slipped into another's skin and has become the character so completely she sees things differently from the way she normally would.

When working on a particularly tense scene, I often get so involved that later, in reading it, I'm surprised by something I've written. Writing toward the end of a chapter in *Dying to Sing,* I had two men and two women looking down at a body. Quite suddenly, one of the men fainted. It was as much a surprise to me as it was to the characters in the scene.

Writers often talk about their characters taking over the story. Certainly, at times, it seems that they have done so. This is not some paranormal happening, however; it's the writer's subconscious at work.

Sometimes people ask me how many pages they should write in a day, or a couple of hours, or whatever writing time they are able to set aside. There's no way for me to answer this question. No two writers are alike and I rarely know how many pages *I* write in a session. I know only that I work all day, with a break for lunch. Once in a while, I feel the need for a cup of coffee or a container of yogurt to keep me going. The telephone rings. I answer it. I pause for such interruptions, because I've never felt it was necessary to isolate myself from my world. I find it easy to slide back into my fictional world as soon as such interruptions are over.

I don't set a specific number of pages a day unless I am getting very close to deadline and won't make it otherwise. Sometimes I've written more than twenty pages in a day, but there are days—more than I care to remember—when I've produced only two.

Don't worry about such statistics; there are no rigid rules. You will find your own working rhythm as you go along. If you really want to write, you will write—regularly and persistently.

One question many beginning writers ask me is whether I write the first draft of my novel all the way through and then revise, or rewrite as I go along. I think the first method is preferable. As the King of Hearts told the White Rabbit in *Alice's Adventures in Wonderland,* "Begin at the beginning and go on till you come to the end: then stop."

Nothing to it, right? Within a fairly short time you can have your whole book down on paper or disk or both. What a wonderful feeling of satisfaction! You've written it, finished it, survived; it's there for you to see—*your* novel. All you have to do now is revise and rewrite it, and rewriting is *much* easier than writing.

Unfortunately, that method, even though I

think it preferable, is not my method. I've tried to write the whole book straight through in rough draft—I really have. But inevitably, as I leave Chapter One to tackle Chapter Two, voices start clamoring in my head. "You've got too much description in the beginning." "Wait a minute! What about the villain? Shouldn't you at least mention his name fairly early?" "Did you accidentally change the color of Jamie's eyes? Did you say brown when you meant green? Don't you think you'd better check?"

And so on. Relentlessly.

The voices get louder and louder until I finally sigh and go back and revise and rewrite Chapter One until those voices are silenced.

When I'm satisfied that Chapter One is as good as I can get it *for the moment,* then and only then can I go on with Chapter Two. After I've rewritten Chapter Two, I usually go back and have another go at chapter One. About the time I reach Chapter Five, I may decide the whole thing isn't moving well, and I go back to Chapter One and start checking the pacing to that point, revising as I go. So it goes, one step forward, five or six back, all the way through.

One advantage to my method, possibly the only advantage, is that when I finish the final chapter, I don't have a lot of rewriting to do.

The disadvantage—a big one—is that it seems as if I'm not making any progress. As I usually have a deadline, this thought makes me start up out of my sleep at three o'clock in the morning with perspiration on my brow. But after twenty some years, I have to accept the fact that this is my method, and I'm stuck with it.

One writer told me years ago that he always writes with the intention of making his first draft the final draft. He aims for about 200 words a day, each sentence honed to perfection in his mind before he puts it down on paper. He does not revise—or so he says. I am in awe of such a writer, though I'm not sure I believe him.

I know a very successful writer who makes sure his calendar is clear for two months, then he goes into his office with a substantial outline and emerges only to eat or sleep until his first draft is done. He doesn't answer his phone, go out to eat, socialize, go to the movies, or read other people's books during this period. Once the first draft is done, he relaxes and takes up his normal life again and spends several hours a day on revisions.

Some writers write whatever scene appeals to them on a particular day, without worrying where it will go in the final version of the novel. Obviously, they must eventually put the scenes in the right order and connect them with transitions.

You can certainly try these various methods and see which one works best for you.

Usually, by the time I sit in front of an empty screen and type Chapter One, I know what the first scene is going to be. I had to know that much in order to start writing the synopsis.

I always try to write in scenes, presenting my story so that the reader will be with me in that place, watching and listening to what's going on. A scene is a complete unit. Characters come together, in conflict or desire or for mutual aid. They talk, they act, they react.

Here is part of the first scene from my novel, *Double Take:*

> Standing unnaturally still so she wouldn't wrinkle the train of her wedding gown, Danielle smiled through her veil at her father's distinguished-looking but glum reflection in the tall, triple mirrors of the church's changing room. "Lighten up, Pops. This is my wedding day, not my funeral."
>
> Harris Kelsey sighed. "I hate sounding like a disgruntled father, but I have to admit I'm not exactly thrilled about you marrying Jonathan Falkirk. I'm not sure he's right for you."
>
> Danielle's stomach coiled in a familiar knot but she managed to speak lightly. "You haven't approved of any man I've ever gone out with."
>
> He smiled wryly. "True. But I'm still going to stick my neck out and ask if you're quite sure Jon is the right man for you."
>
> About to say "Of course" she hesitated, wondering why his question had aroused a feeling of panic, a feeling that there was some memory wanting to come into her mind, a memory she couldn't possibly allow.

Without exception, my first scene is a scene in which something is going to change for my main character or characters. He or she will meet someone, or lose someone, or find a body, or learn of a situation that will affect his or her life. This day in the main character's life will not be the same as any other day. In the above example, Danielle is about to find out that her fiancé has not shown up at the church and has changed his mind about getting married.

In my early days as a writer, I read and was told over and over that I should always start my stories or novels with a narrative hook. I had a mental image of a kind of shepherd's crook pulling the reader into the story, the way stage managers used to haul unsuccessful comedians off the vaudeville stage.

It wasn't a bad image, I suppose, but it made me think I had to come up with a beginning paragraph that was terribly dramatic and exciting, if not sensational. Many beginning writers have this idea, and sometimes a dramatic and exciting beginning is called for. More often, however, what is needed is just something *interesting*. Interesting enough, that is, to engage the attention of a reader, keeping in mind that the first reader whom you must appeal to is an *editor*, without whose approval that paragraph won't get published.

You can begin with anything at all: a situation, two characters interacting, talking, making love, fighting, cooking. You can even begin with your setting, if the setting is interesting enough—a haunted house, a battlefield, a storm at sea. But remember that your first paragraph *must* lead the reader into the story, and *it should have something to do with the story*. This may seem obvious, but you'd be surprised how many beginners' manuscripts start out with a very exciting scene that has absolutely nothing to do with the rest of the novel. A man witnesses a terrible accident on the way to work. He goes on to his office, and then the story begins. The accident has nothing to do with the character or the subsequent story; it was used only to provide a narrative hook.

Worse than this, in my opinion, is a narrative hook that appears to put the main character or characters in dreadful danger, getting the reader all steamed up, and then the whole scene turns out to be a dream. A pox on all such trickery!

Have you ever watched someone choose a novel in a bookstore? Unless the person is looking for a book by a known author, he or she will usually be attracted by the cover or title. Taking the book from the rack, the reader will glance at the front and back covers, perhaps scan the blurb on the back and the blurb in the front, then read the first paragraph.

Most authors can't do much about the cover design or artwork or the blurbs, which are prepared by the staff of the publishing house, but if your prospective reader reads the first paragraph and puts your book back on the shelf, you have no one but yourself to blame.

When people turn on a television set, they expect instant picture, instant sound. They have also come to expect instant gratification from a novel. However, if you haven't come up with a really good first paragraph for your novel, don't despair. Just begin! Don't spend hours staring at your computer screen or a blank page thinking up a first sentence; just make one up and go on from there. If necessary, a better idea will come along. It may even be that the sentence you typed just to get the story going will turn out to be exactly right after all.

Take a look at novels in the library or bookstore to see how other authors began. You're not going to copy anyone, of course, but sometimes reading other writers' work will trigger *original* ideas for you to use.

Here are a few of my own first sentences:

The patrol car nosed quietly into the parking lot behind the Mountain View shopping center.

There was a feeling of excitement, of celebration, in the late-afternoon air of Quebec City.

The long gleaming car seemed to appear out of nowhere.

The engagement of the eminent plastic surgeon, Dr. Philip Talbot, to Kristi Johanssen, the nationally known model, was announced on Friday, May 25th, in the View section of the *Los Angeles Times*.

He boarded the plane in Chicago.

Bougainvillea cascaded over the high walls of the court-yard, so brilliantly scarlet against the light-colored adobe that Blythe was almost blinded when she looked down at the wedding party on the terrace steps.

It wasn't a bad feeling, rather like drifting; she was shrinking away from the borders that defined her body, dwindling into a shining molecule.

It was happening again.

My mother never did like men.

None of these openings is particularly exciting, and certainly, none would compare with Dickens's opening to *A Tale of Two Cities*. But as you read each one, did you wonder what the next sentence would be? If you did, then these are good first sentences.

Each of those openings had a great deal to do with the plot. The patrol car was about to be dispatched to a crime scene that would set in motion a chain of events that affected everyone in the story, including one of the police officers. The long gleaming car was driven by a man who almost forced the heroine off the road; later he falls in love with her. The engagement of Philip and Kristi caused a badly disturbed individual to snap and to plan Kristi's death. The fact that the heroine's mother "never did like men" had a great deal to do with the solution to the mystery.

Of course, there is a lot more to a first chapter than the first sentence, but no matter how good the rest of it is, if you don't draw readers in with that first sentence and paragraph and page, they might not read on to get to the good part.

On the bulletin board in my office there are several quotes that I live by. One (unfortunately I do not know the source) is this: *No reader ever waited in suspense for the suspense to begin.*

Here is the most important thing I can tell you about the beginning of a novel. *You don't have to tell your reader everything at once.* Probably the single most common flaw I have seen in many beginners' novels is their attempt to cram too much information into the first chapter. The story doesn't get underway until page five, or even Chapter Two. In the meantime, the heroine or hero is walking along in the countryside or on a city street or sitting on a train or an airplane. (An airplane is a favorite with beginners. Another well-worn opening has a heroine sitting in a bubble bath.) While the character is thus engaged, he or she is thinking about everything that has happened in his or her life up to that moment.

Yawn.

Sometimes, instead of thinking, the character *muses*. If you ever find yourself typing the words "He (or she) mused," immediately launch a rewriting attack.

Sometimes a writer will introduce so many characters at the beginning that the reader gets lost trying to keep up with them. In the first three pages of *The Man of Property* (Book I of *The Forsyte Saga*), John Galsworthy introduced sixteen characters and gave a mini-description of each. He won the Nobel Prize for literature. But John Galsworthy was a genius, and the power of his writing alone is sufficient to hold the reader's interest.

Huge amounts of information aren't necessary at the outset of a novel. They will slow down the pace of the storyline. As the writer, *you* need to know everything there is to know about your characters, but you don't need to tell the reader all of it at once.

Instead, *show* your reader one or two or a few characters in action against their setting, making *brief* references to any information that is absolutely essential. As the novel progresses, you can weave in other essential facts through dialogue. Let the reader *gradually* learn the characters' backgrounds in a natural way.

When we meet new people, we don't get to know all there is to know about them right away. In spite of this, we usually decide fairly quickly whether or not we like or admire or dislike or distrust them. We make such decisions based on what they say, how they say it, and on their body language. Choice of clothing, grooming, and whether attitudes are generally negative or positive are other clues to personality and character traits.

As time goes by, we get to know people better and confirm or modify our initial impressions. The reader will do the same if you weave in these clues to personality for your characters at appropriate places in the novel.

The ancient Romans had a phrase for how to begin a novel: *in medias res*. Into the midst of things. That's where your beginning should plunge your readers. Something is happening. Someone is talking or shouting or arguing. Somebody is *doing* something with, to, about, or in spite of, someone else.

At the same time, your readers also need to know *where* the story is taking place, the background and setting, and whether it is in the present or past. Preferably right off. I hate reading several pages of a novel without knowing if I'm indoors or outdoors, in this century or another. Just as nature abhors a vacuum, so does a reader's mind. If you don't provide *some* clues to setting and characters and period, readers will fill them in subconsciously. I've had the experience of thinking that an opening scene in a manuscript is taking place on board ship, only to discover the characters are actually in a restaurant.

I also dislike reading several pages of opening dialogue without knowing something about the people who are speaking.

Remember that clarity is important in all elements of writing. Writing is communication. Communication requires clarity. And nowhere does a novel require clarity as much as in the beginning. If readers cannot visualize what's going on, they will not continue reading your novel. And no writer wants that to happen.

So then, introduce your main characters—or minor characters or whoever's going to get your story rolling—*in action*. Give readers an indication of setting without bogging them down with a lot of details. If your novel starts in a kitchen, unless it has truly remarkable features important to the story or to the characters, there's usually no need to mention that it has a stove and a refrigerator. The reader responds to the word "kitchen" with a mental image and will supply the rest of the setting without even realizing it.

If your story starts out in a tavern or a cave in the side of a hill, let the reader know. Briefly. Succinctly. Get the story off to a good start by thinking, "Lights, camera, action." Pace, *the rate of movement or progress,* is something to watch out for constantly. Sometimes your story will move along at a fast trot, perhaps even a gallop; sometimes it will slow down to a walk. Be sure the pace fits the action.

There's no rule about where the beginning ends and the middle starts. I have heard writers state emphatically the number of pages each section should take, but I've never been able to work in such a mechanical way. When I'm writing I don't even think, consciously, "This is the end of the beginning and now I'm starting on the middle." I just try to get my story off to a good start and keep it going through the middle to the end.

◄ 8 ►

Transitions and Flashbacks

Transitions link your scenes and chapters: They signify a shift from one subject or place or time or character to another. For example, a familiar transition, which of course you will never use, is: *Meanwhile, back at the ranch....*

Try to avoid ending scenes or chapters with a character going to sleep, which is not only trite; there's also a danger that if the characters go to sleep the reader will do likewise! Something *interesting* or intriguing should be happening at the end of a scene or chapter. It's a good idea to study novels to see how other writers handle scenes and transitions.

Here are two paragraphs that constitute a transition, from the beginning of Chapter Five of *Shadow of a Doubt:*

After making the rounds of taverns and restaurants, guided by Derry's matchbooks and coasters, Turner and Jamie stopped at an historic house and a carriage museum. The caretaker at the museum and one bartender recognized Derry's cap, but had no memory of anything else connected with him.

Climbing on foot up a steep street to an old fort that now housed a restaurant and bar, Jamie was tired, sweaty and definitely discouraged.

Immediately following that transition, the scene begins:

"This is not going well," Jamie said after they had settled themselves on stools at the fairly busy bar and had ordered drinks.

Turner grunted a vague answer. Ever since they'd come into the bar, he'd been glancing around furtively, as if he was looking for something . . . or someone.

Sipping her mineral water, Jamie looked at the high ceilings and whitewashed walls. The place was lit by a wagon wheel full of electric light bulbs. There were several flags hanging from the rafters.

A woman entered the bar and Turner glanced at her, then away. "Are you expecting someone?" Jamie asked.

He had just raised his glass to his lips. The clear sparkling liquid sloshed but didn't spill. "I'm just keeping an eye on things," he said. A lame answer if ever she'd heard one.

"Ready for another?" the barmaid asked.

They both shook their heads, then Jamie dug out Derry's photograph and laid it on the bar.

The scene continues with the barmaid telling Jamie and Turner all she knows about Derry and includes information about the woman (Linda) whose entrance had caught Turner's interest. Turner decides to question Linda, and the scene and chapter end like this, in Turner's viewpoint:

Linda's body language had given rise to another question. She'd been horrified right until the moment he turned the photo over. Whose photo had she expected it to be?

The next chapter begins with an abrupt transition in place:

Along with eight or so tourists, Turner and Jamie boarded the *Coral Queen* at the ferry terminal in Hamilton.

Sometimes it works better to make a transition by shifting point of view: After presenting a scene in one person's viewpoint, you can switch to another person's viewpoint for the next. Or you can make a transition in time: *Three days later . . .*

Avoid making your transitions too lengthy. If two characters—Pamela and her mom—have had a quarrel, and you end the scene with Pamela stomping out of the room, you don't have to show her closing the door, climbing the stairs to her room. Just write: "In her bedroom, Pamela . . ." or skip that too and jump to the next day, or the next week.

In some cases, you don't need a transition at all. You can just hop or slide from one scene to another, as in these two paragraphs from *Double Take*:

That wasn't the only reason she'd accepted Steff's invitation, she realized as she hung up the phone. She'd felt . . . off-center somehow, since seeing Adrian on Tuesday, as though she'd behaved badly where he was concerned.

But how else could she have behaved? She'd *had* to discourage him. It wasn't his fault she kept confusing him with Jon, of course, but the fact was there and there wasn't much either one of them could do about it.

Steff was a wonderful cook. The mingled smells of garlic and onion greeted Dani at the front door. "Coq au vin," Steff announced as she tossed Dani's jacket onto a chair.

Leaving extra space on the page between these paragraphs alerts the reader to the abrupt change.

As you continue writing in scenes and transitions and narrative passages, you flesh out your plot and bring it and the characters to life for your readers. Throughout your novel, try to create pictures in the reader's mind, using *only* those details that show character as well as appearance, atmosphere or weather as well as setting.

Sensory details are very important. You have five senses—use all of them in writing your novel. Make your scenes come alive with sights and sounds and smells wherever possible—briefly, but succinctly. Here's an example—the description of an underground cave—from *Shadow of a Doubt*:

Fantastically shaped stalagmites thrust upward through the water and from shelflike formations in the limestone walls. It was an awe-inspiring display, mysterious and slightly scary. The air smelled overused as though it had been inhaled and exhaled by too many people. Water dripped constantly. Jamie shivered in her shorts and cotton shirt as she looked up at stalactite "daggers" aimed straight at her head.

Count how many senses I used in that paragraph, which went through several rewrites before this final version. I was trying for a certain atmosphere. A couple of paragraphs later, Jamie is going to discover a body.

If possible, intersperse sensory details that describe the setting in the background of an interesting scene that has a lot of action. Make every scene work to advance the story, develop the characters, show the setting, intrigue the reader enough to make him or her turn the page.

Symbols, used sparingly and with freshness, can also make your writing more powerful, if you don't make them too complicated. If the reader has to strain to work out the connection, you've overdone it.

Symbols can also be used to connect past to present. In one of my novels, the hero wears a cowboy hat that belonged to his father, who died when his house caught fire. The cowboy hat was the *only* possession of the father that was saved and the hero wore it all the time because to him it *symbolized* his father.

Perhaps a carpet bag could be handed down through three generations. It and its contents may provide a clue to the solution of a murder and also have a profound effect on the life of the last person to receive it.

A character in your novel could be afraid of heights because, when he was a small boy living in the country, he had to walk across a high bridge above a river between his home and school. The bridge could become symbolic of the turmoil in the man's life, and foreshadow the ending in which he returns to his home and jumps from the middle of the span into the canyon below.

Such a story might begin with the man standing on the bridge, contemplating suicide, and reliving the past events that have led him to this desperate point.

I am reluctant to talk about flashback scenes because I don't like to use flashbacks and if possible avoid them. But sometimes they are necessary and you really need to know the basic techniques of moving back and forth in time.

Suppose your character, Marlene, is walking along a cliff path in the rain, and you want to relate some relevant past events in her life. Although you are writing in Marlene's viewpoint, you should not simply *tell* the reader what happened at a previous time: You need to show it dramatically.

It might go something like this:

> "It had been raining that day, too. Harder than this. Marlene had run into the library to escape the sudden downpour and there was Leland, sitting in front of a computer, his back ramrod straight as usual.
>
> She'd put her hand on his shoulder. "Leland," she said. "How come you're not working at the bank today?"
>
> Obviously startled, Leland swung around. "I'm not . . . I wasn't supposed to . . . I'm sick."
>
> He didn't *look* sick. He looked *nervous*.

The scene goes on, with Marlene questioning Leland and becoming more and more suspicious of the reason for his absence from the bank.

Leading into the flashback, use a few "hads," indicating the past perfect tense, as I did in the above example. This moves the time sequences from simple past tense, in which most story action takes place, to the past perfect tense. Once you've established the earlier time in the scene, omit the "hads" and use regular past tense again. For example: "'Leland,' Marlene *said*." And "Leland *swung* around."

On the way out of the scene, use "hads" again until you are back in the "present."

> "That's the whole story," Leland said. "I would never lie to you, Marlene."
>
> She had believed him. He had seemed so troubled, so sincere. She hadn't known his whole story was a lie until the local newspaper published a full account of Leland's fraudulent bookkeeping.
>
> What a fool she had been, she thought, gazing down at the turbulent sea.

Be sure the time covered in the flashback can be accounted for in the present. In the example above, I have Marlene hiking along a cliff path as the reader learns about Leland. Probably a half an hour at the most would pass in this flashback, so the reader will accept the fact that Marlene could be hiking for that long.

Many beginning writers, and some established ones, fall into the trap of having the flashback take place while the viewpoint character is, say, climbing the steps to his apartment. The flashback might cover an hour, a week, even a year of time, and at the end of it, the character is just reaching the top of the steps. Readers might well wonder how anyone could climb steps this slowly.

I wrote one flashback recently in which the viewpoint character, nicknamed Fairy, is drinking tea and remembering her friend Bliss *telling* her about the man in her life:

> Growing up, Fairy and Bliss had talked hour after hour about love. They had expected so much from love. Too much. Even poor old Stubby hadn't quite managed to come up to Fairy's expectations, though he'd given it a valiant go. Prince Charming himself would have been hard pressed to fulfill expectations fed by films of the thirties and forties.
>
> *Love.* Setting down her cup, Fairy hummed along as she heard Bliss's soprano voice singing sweetly across more than fifty years.
>
> *As Time Goes By.*
>
> "It's our song, Fairy," Bliss had said. "Paul's and mine. You should hear Paul sing it. You *will* hear Paul sing it. He's coming to Penmorton next week. He's coming to be with me."
>
> Even after all these years Fairy could recall every detail Bliss had told her. Every scene was as clear as if it had been made into a film by Mr. J. Arthur Rank. She could feel the sun shining warm on her head just as if she'd been there. She could smell the salty air, hear the tumbling roar of the surf, as Bliss Penberthy and Paul Carmichael walked out together in Penmorton on a beautiful sunny day.

I used several flashbacks in the novel, *As Years Go By,* because it is a double love story that takes place in the present as well as in the past.

Instead of using flashbacks, I usually prefer to make brief references to the past in dialogue, or in a character's thoughts. When you use a flashback, be sure it is required for clarity, doesn't interrupt your story, and provides a *necessary* link between past and present events.

◄ 9 ►

Presenting Your Characters

By the time I begin the actual writing of a novel, I know my characters pretty well; they even interrupt my sleep to talk to me. At this point I can see them, and I want my reader to see them. There are writers who feel it's never necessary to give details of a character's appearance. They say that if the character is an artist, or a bank manager, or a police officer, or a cowboy, or a fireman, or an accountant, the reader will visualize that person.

This is all true, but I think novelists should show readers people and places as *they* see them. This does not mean you should stop the story for a page or two while you list all the details of a character's appearance. In movies or plays, characters don't stop on stage while the playwright or screenwriter describes them. The characters join the action and the viewer takes in the details of their appearance. In a novel, you *can* stop the action for a paragraph or two, but it's best to take no longer than that to present a character. At the same time, any description should do more than show the character, it should also give a hint of what the person is like.

In writing *Dying to Sing,* the first novel in my mystery series, I worked out in my mind the details of heroine Charlie Plato's appearance:

Physical details: She's thirty, has orange hair, green eyes. She's tall and lean. She eats right, and heartily. She works out with weight machines.

Character details: She's outspoken, sassy, straight-forward, honest, nosy, doesn't trust men but loves them anyway.

History: She's been married once, to a gynecologist. She loved her husband, but couldn't stand his womanizing. She now has no family except for a pet rabbit.

The mystery series is written in first person through Charlie's viewpoint. This is the most difficult viewpoint in which to describe the main character, because you, the writer, are telling this story through her eyes, and she can't see herself unless she looks in a mirror, which is the worst cliché there is.

Having another character describe Charlie—perhaps her partner Zack Hunter—wouldn't work, since the whole book is told from Charlie's point of view; I'd have to have Zack do it through dialogue. As he looked at her hair, he might say, "Is that a white hair I see in your orange mop?" And then later she might stride along beside him, showing the reader that she had long legs. Her good eating habits and lean build would gradually be revealed.

I would *not* let Zack say, "Hey, Charlie, is that a white hair I see in your orange mop? And what about those green eyes? Contacts or your own? How do you stay so darn skinny anyway? And how tall are you, 5'10"?"

A real case of overkill! But I've seen it in print, and it jars me every time.

I prefer to give a quick, straightforward picture of my characters as they appear, then add details to that picture as I go along, also reminding the reader from time to time of some characteristic or other.

Here's how I introduce Charlie on the tenth line of the first page of *Dying to Sing*. She is teaching a line dancing lesson in the country-western bar CHAPS:

> Some of the women, like me, twitched their skinny hips in jeans, others wore shorts and T-shirts or long full skirts. P.J., one of the regulars, whipped her tow-colored ponytail every time she did a quarter turn.
>
> I was envious; my hair doesn't whip. It's long enough, but too frizzy to do more than flop. It's also orange. Not strawberry blond or red or titan. Orange as in carrot. Orange as in pumpkin. I'm Charlie Plato, by the way, a thirty-year-old divorcée with an attitude. In other words, depending on your point of view, a nineties woman or a walking cliché.

Note that there's a broad hint to Charlie's character here. It's pretty clear that she is not conceited and doesn't take herself too seriously, but she's not going to put up with any nonsense.

The other characters are all seen through Charlie's eyes. She mentions Zack several times before he actually shows up. This is how she describes him when he first appears on scene:

> Zack Hunter, as you know if you haven't lived in a cave for the last few years, is 6'2" tall, 35 years old, tough-looking in a lean, rangy, breath-stopping, sexy sort of way. He has thick black hair that always looks boyishly tousled, a lined forehead, a slightly crooked, once-broken never-quite-fixed nose and hard green eyes that are permanently narrowed as if he's squinting into a dust storm. He also has a jagged scar on his left cheek, which according to Zack was bestowed upon him by a bull's horn.
>
> Sure it was.
>
> For non-TV watchers, if there are any such, I'll explain that for seven years Zack Hunter played Sheriff Lazarro on the wildly popular, totally improbable hit series, *Prescott's Landing*.

Go through some novels in the library to see how other writers present character. Whenever I come across characters in a novel who seem truly real to me, I go back to see how the author brought the characters to life, how he or she made them appear to be real people with real emotions. Characters should of course have emotions, but they don't have to emote all over the place. If something affects them, however, show them reacting emotionally to what occurs. In a novel, as in life, people feel love, hatred, fear, envy, jealousy, etc. Whenever possible, *show* what they feel by the way they act or react.

Real people make gestures, rake a hand through their hair, shrug, etc. Mouths tighten with anger, eyes narrow with suspicion. Authors use such gestures to reveal character to their readers. An old man might pull on one ear before speaking. If this isn't used too often, it could be effective. You can stress one feature several times during the course of a novel—the way a character frowns when thinking, for instance. The trick is not to overdo it.

Character and emotion can be revealed not only by what people do, but by what they say. Which brings us to dialogue.

Have you ever had the experience of meeting a person who seemed truly attractive, but then said something that made you hopping mad? Characters in a story don't really come alive until they talk. The way they talk, the things they say, should help the reader know them better, and should also have something to do with the story. *Everything* in a story should have something to do with the storyline.

Try to avoid aimless dialogue—talk for the sake of talking. In real life we all do a lot of this and have a tendency to tune out other people's aimless talk if it doesn't interest us. We repeat ourselves, wander off the subject, contradict ourselves, say far too much about dull subjects like the weather.

In writing novels, you must make your dialogue

crisp and relevant to the story, and let it reveal
your characters.

Here's an example of dialogue from *Shadow of
a Doubt*. Jamie (an American tourist in Bermuda
to investigate her friend's death) is having break-
fast in her hotel with the manager, Charles
Hollingsworth, an English Bermudian. We're in
Jamie's viewpoint:

> Jamie felt out of place in such surroundings. Her hair
> was still damp, she hadn't had a chance to put makeup
> on, and she should probably have worn the one dress she'd
> brought with her. No, that wasn't possible—it was only
> an hour since she'd pulled it out of her duffel and hung it
> on the back of the bathroom door, hoping the steam from
> successive showers would remove the creases. Meticulous
> and organized in her business life, Jamie tended to be
> relaxed in private. Messy, her mother said.
> "This is a lovely hotel," she said awkwardly.
> "We think so," Charles said. "We draw a distinguished
> clientele. The gentleman over there, for example, is a ma-
> jor European financier. Very, very wealthy. His wife—you
> may recognize her—is Lucia Ugo, the opera diva. And
> just beyond them the Honorable Mr. and Mrs. Warrender,
> sitting with Mrs. John Rossiter, board chair of the
> Kleber Museum."
> Jamie was glad to see her omelet arrive. None of these
> names meant a thing to her, but she tried her best to look
> impressed in deference to the respectful tone of Hol-
> lingsworth's voice.

By the end of this passage, the reader has
learned something about Charles's character, and
Jamie's. This scene might seem quite unrelated
to the story, but later Charles turns out to have

been very much involved in Jamie's friend's death—and his snobbishness is part of his motivation. If Charles hadn't been important to the plot, I would not have let Jamie spend this much time with him.

Dialogue is of extreme importance in revealing character, furthering the plot in an interesting way, and keeping up the pace of the story. Just about every word of dialogue should have something to do with the story.

One of the reasons I've included that fairly large chunk of dialogue from *Shadow of a Doubt* is to illustrate other important points that have to do with dialogue.

If you have imagined your characters fully, if they are three-dimensional in your mind, you will *hear* them speak. Getting what they say down on paper is not easy. I tend to write it down the way I "hear" it, then go back later and edit it, taking out all words that aren't really necessary. The main thing is to try to be brief. Charles's speech in that passage is probably one of the longest in *Shadow of a Doubt*. It was important not because it showed the setting—though it did that—but because it revealed a facet of his character.

Charles was speaking with an English accent, by the way. My aim when I'm depicting any speech is to use the speech patterns that an English or French or Japanese or American person, or other nationality, would use. Within those nationalities there are several different types of speech, so I try to capture those differences, too.

In *Shadow of a Doubt,* several characters speak British English, but they don't all sound alike. Charles Hollingsworth's speech is that of a well-educated, cultured Englishman. By contrast, here's the skipper of a glass-bottomed boat, also English:

> "Hello ducks, what can I do for you?"
> "I thought I might use some of the sun block you mentioned earlier," Jamie said.
> "You don't need to worry, you've a good tan. I like your titfer, by the way."
> "My what?"
> "Tit for tat—hat. Cockney rhyming slang, ducks."

This is about as far as I go in using dialect. There's no point in using so much dialect that readers have to sound out words to figure out what they mean. An occasional word to indicate the flavor of the language—such as "ducks," used by the British as a term of endearment—is all that's necessary, with perhaps a comment from the viewpoint character that the person has a strong English accent, or French, or whatever.

Do avoid misspelling words to indicate dialect. This can be very distracting to the reader—"wot" instead of "what," for example.

In the example above, the skipper's use of cockney rhyming slang added a note of humor, which is always a plus. He is altogether a cheery sort of person, until Jamie starts asking him questions about her friend's drowning.

The main thing to be aware of is that each character is an individual, with distinctive speech patterns. One character should not sound like another—or like you.

Now, a word about "he said" and "she said."

Ignore lists of "said" substitutes. "He said" and "she said" are simple, and preferable to most of their synonyms, such as "he articulated" or "she asserted." The reader's eye slides over "he said" or "she said" without being conscious of them, though they do help the reader keep track of who is talking.

This should not be taken to mean that it's O.K. to write "he said" or "she said" *every* time anyone speaks. Such constant repetition would be extremely irritating to the reader. Yes, of course, you can use an occasional "he answered," "she shouted," "he murmured," but in moderation.

If you have a long passage of dialogue between two people, you can write several exchanges without using "said" or a substitute. Or instead of using "said," you can indicate who is speaking before he or she speaks. The following conversation between Jamie and Turner in *Shadow of a Doubt* illustrates each of these methods:

"Loretta did lie about the suitcase," Jamie said. "If she would lie for someone, maybe she'd break into a room for someone."

"Rex, you mean."

"If he's the chief. Or someone else if he's not."

Turner looked at her with great interest. "Who do you have in mind?"

"I didn't care much for Gordon Stacey."

Turner laughed shortly. "I don't care for him myself, Jamie, but he's a terribly upright citizen. It's a bit of a stretch to imagine he could be involved in running drugs."

"He's a part owner of the Victoria Hotel," Jamie said.

I don't use and don't like such reversals as "said she," or "said Charles," or "said the tall man." I've never heard anyone use that construction when *telling* a story, except in a jocular way—"says you!"

One of the best methods for bringing a character to life is to try to get inside the character, the way an actor does. Preparing for his role as the evil Nazi Commander in the movie *Schindler's List,* Ralph Fiennes studied Nazi S.S. recruitment films and read interviews with Holocaust survivors. He also worked with a voice coach to achieve an Austrian accent and put on twenty-six pounds.

Writers can learn a lot from actors. Instead of *creating* characters, we need to learn how to *become* our characters. I cannot write about an eighteen-year-old boy or a ninety-year-old man or a thirty-year-old woman from *my* viewpoint. I have to become that person and look out at the world through that person's eyes.

Think of how an actor becomes a character. He adopts a certain way of walking, of talking, of moving, of thinking. He uses gestures, language, facial expressions to convey this character to his audience. He thinks about that character's personality and history and lets that knowledge determine his presentation of the character.

Show, don't tell. Sometimes this advice is taken too literally. There will be times when it's better to use narrative. What the maxim means is, don't write, "Marcie was happy." Pretend you're an actress. Get inside happy Marcie. What is she doing? Dancing around gleefully? Or is she more introverted? Is she sitting quietly but with glowing eyes?

Which is better: "Jamie was shocked," or "Jamie felt the blood drain from her face"? "He looked drunk," or "He peered at her owlishly, breathing rum in her face"?

I have a lot of fun with minor characters. I try to avoid stereotypes, even in a character who appears in only one paragraph. A landlady reads tea leaves, and advises the heroine on her love life; an elderly lady has a wicked sense of humor and runs on the beach in a Spandex jogging suit.

Clothing and appearance can characterize. Here's a young man who is wearing a ragged flannel shirt and blue jeans with deliberate rips in the knees. He has an earring in his left ear, whiskers sprouting in patches from his chin, long straggly hair. I know a young man who has a collection of T-shirts with messages that all declaim he was "born to be bad." The teenage girl who wears a bustier and a thigh-high leather skirt is not at all like the teenage girl who wears skirts down to her calves and blouses with lace collars.

Food choice can characterize, as can music choice, grooming habits, cleanliness or sloppiness. The car a character drives—pickup truck or Mercedes, or old and cherished Mustang—tells readers a lot and may reflect his financial status. The way the character's home is furnished also characterizes him. Does he own the house, or rent an apartment? Is the house part of a duplex? Is it a townhouse or a country cottage? All are characterizing details.

Creating characters, *becoming* characters, is great fun. Practice it. It's one part of writing that does get easier with experience.

◀ 10 ▶

Knowing When to Stop

THE END.
My favorite words. I've done it again. For a while there I wasn't sure I could make it, but here it is. *The End.*

Well, not quite. As with everything else in writing, a certain amount of checking is necessary. One of the most important things to remember while writing the ending is that change is *vital* in every novel. Whatever has happened in the story should have had some *impact,* some *effect* on the situation and the characters involved. In other words, by the end of your novel, your main characters must have *changed* from what they were in the beginning; the initial situation must also have changed; or the main characters' attitude toward the situation must have changed.

To ensure a strong ending, your main characters must have acted to bring about a change in the initial situation or problem. Don't rely on coincidence, or fate, or what the Greeks call *deus ex machina*—a god out of a machine—to resolve the story. In the final outcome, whether the main characters win or lose, whether their change is for the better or for the worse, they should have been actively *involved* in bringing about that change, rather than simply bemoaning their fate while things happen *to* them.

If the causes and effects in your novel are in the proper sequence, the middle will flow into the ending, and the ending will be logical. It must *not* be predictable. There should be enough conflict and suspense throughout the novel to create uncertainty about the outcome. Maybe things *won't* work out. Maybe the murderer will *not* be caught; maybe Thomas will *not* wake from the coma; maybe Jill *won't* find true love; maybe Karrell will *lose* the battle with the Selacians and earth will be destroyed.

The ending must also be *believable*. If a man has behaved brutally toward his wife all the way through your story, it will be difficult for readers to accept an ending in which he has suddenly seen the error of his ways and changed into a lovable guy.

The ending must tie up loose ends, yet leave a feeling that much more could and will happen in the future to these fascinating people, whom (if you've done your job well) readers will think about long after turning the last page.

If you can come up with a surprise ending that meets all of these criteria, then by all means use it. There should be some surprise in any ending. Or at least, some part of it should be unexpected.

But you have to be careful not to sacrifice believability for surprise.

Most novels have several storylines or threads going through them, as in my novel, *Beyond the Rainbow:*

Philip and Kristi are unhappy in their marriage.

Philip's half-brother Gareth resents their marriage.

Philip's mother hates Kristi.

Philip's sister doesn't approve of Kristi.

Gareth's old friend, who is gay, will do anything for Gareth.

Someone is trying to kill Kristi.

This novel was very complicated and had several other threads, but these should suffice for illustration. All of these threads wound in and out of each other throughout the novel. Each of them needed to reach a convincing solution at the end. The old friend attempted suicide. Gareth died. Kristi and Philip came no nearer to solving their problems, but they had both changed in several ways and were willing to *try* to save their marriage. The last couple of lines were:

> "Please don't stop loving me, Philip," Kristi said shakily. It was almost a promise. It was at least a beginning.

The ending of your story is every bit as important as the beginning. If readers didn't like the beginning, they won't read to the end. If they aren't satisfied by the ending, they won't be inclined to buy your next book.

Don't write an unhappy ending for any novel because you think that will make it more literary. It won't. One of the things I've noticed in reading beginners' novels is that the endings almost always tend to be downbeat. If you are going to kill everyone off in your stories, be sure it's necessary. Most people read novels for entertainment, for escape. If it's necessary to the integrity of the story for a number of people to die, then die they must. But if it's not absolutely crucial, why not let one or two people live and be happy?

In most novels, there is some point toward the end when everything seems bleak for the protagonist. Traditionally, this is called "the black moment." It's always darkest before the dawn, goes the old cliché. Like most clichés, it is usually true:

- The wagons are trapped in the canyon. Death is at hand. The cavalry hasn't shown up because the fussbudget of a captain is still cleaning his boots.

- John is walking out. "That's it," he says. "I'm through trying to make you believe in me. Goodbye forever."
Mary sinks down on the stairs, hand to her throat.

- The raiders are positioning themselves to launch their proton torpedoes, which will easily penetrate the battle station's ray-shields and blast it and its occupants into the be-all and end-all.

- The judge raps his gavel for silence in court. "You are going to jail for the rest of your natural life," he tells the shivering prisoner at the bar.

If you do decide to include a black moment, make sure it arises naturally and logically out of what has come before:

> Jamie watched as Turner walked toward the *Kiskadee,* closely followed by Kyle. His head was up, his lean figure militarily straight. She was quite sure that he was thinking through all possible plans for them to escape, but at the moment, with Kyle walking almost on his heels, his hand alertly tucked over the gun he'd stuck in his jeans pocket, Turner Garrett looked very helpless indeed. So helpless that Jamie's heart seemed to swell as she watched him . . .
>
> If anything happened to Turner, she would never know happiness again. If she happened to survive herself. Which seemed doubtful.
>
> "Our turn," Hokins said, getting out of the car . . .
>
> . . . He put an arm around her shoulders, keeping his free hand, with his gun, in his shorts pocket. Jamie shuddered away from his touch. This man had killed Derry. And Anna.
>
> "What are you planning to do with us?" she asked, keeping her voice even.
>
> He laughed. "We're going to kill you, sweetheart," he said.

This is indisputably a black moment. But I didn't deliberately *plan* a black moment for *Shadow of a Doubt;* it just arose, logically, it seemed to me, from the preceding events. Perhaps the best way to handle the black moment is not to plan on it until the novel is written; then when you revise, check to make sure it's there.

After the black moment, you need to figure out a way for the characters to fight their way out of the seemingly hopeless situation, or be destroyed, depending on the story. Whatever action the characters take, you must have prepared for it earlier in the story. A sentence like, "Gathering all his strength, Bart leaped over the nine-foot high fence and ran off into the sunset," won't do unless you've already *shown* Bart to be an Olympic-class high jumper.

Endings for romance and mystery novels must meet other requirements besides those already discussed. Readers expect romance novels to end happily. Quite often, I've heard critics of the genre talk about "formula novels," as though there is some kind of blueprint that can be followed, but I've never known what this "formula" is. Perhaps the word applies to the earlier definition of a romance novel: Boy meets girl, boy loses girl, boy gets girl. Most of today's romance novels are far more complex and varied than that.

However, the romance novel still requires one absolutely necessary ingredient: a happy ending.

The ending must be in doubt, though, or there will be no suspense. Throughout the novel something must happen to prevent this man and this woman from solving whatever problems are keeping them emotionally apart. At the end, this problem must be solved in a convincing, entertaining, and unpredictable way.

In mystery novels, endings are also extremely important. You can't just have your sleuth suddenly slap her forehead and announce she's solved the whole thing, especially if you haven't revealed her step-by-step method of arriving at this solution. You must be sure you have laid out all your clues, planted some red herrings, given the reader all the information the sleuth has, at the same time managing not to identify the murderer. When you finally do reveal who the murderer is, the reader will believe you, because of the clues and information you worked into the novel along the way. But your readers should still be surprised by some aspect of the solution.

You will also have to explain certain things to your readers, and answer questions they'll have on their minds. It used to be acceptable at the end of a mystery for the sleuth to gather all the suspects in a room and explain circumstantial evidence that had led to the correct deductions. This is often still done today with some variations. In skillful hands it can work, or it can be totally boring and long-winded.

One way to avoid this boredom for readers is to clear up most of their questions before the murderer is revealed. If you can do this during an action scene—while the murderer is pointing a gun at the sleuth, for instance—so much the better. The murderer might brag a little about the crime, but beware—if the bragging lasts too long and the murderer goes into too much detail, the readers' willing suspension of disbelief will give way under the strain.

For *all* types of novels, you need to break necessary explanations into several parts, tie up various less important threads as you go along—in believable and possibly surprising ways. *Then* produce the final, believable, but unexpected and unpredictable ending that fully satisfies readers.

None of this is easy.

Be sure you stop when your novel reaches the end. Bow out when your story is over. Put the cover on the typewriter or turn off the computer. Leave.

Years ago, when I was writing a romantic suspense novel set in Japan, I envisioned the last chapter as a wonderfully colorful, traditional Japanese wedding. I had never attended such a wedding, but I had lived in Japan for a couple of years and had read a lot about Japanese customs and ceremonies. In order to be sure I had every detail right, I sent the finished chapter to a Japanese friend in Tokyo, who found that everything was correct.

And then I realized that the story had really ended in the chapter before the wedding. My main characters had settled their differences, the murderer had been unmasked, the family was reunited. I didn't need the wedding after all! So I took it out.

◄ 11 ►

The Pleasures of Revision

In the numerous novel manuscripts by inexperienced writers I've read over the years, I've found that the one—the *only*—thing they had in common, was that they needed more work. Always.

Good writing is the result of rewriting. No writer ever gets a manuscript completely right the first time. I keep refining and rewriting and rethinking until my novel is as good as I can make it. An editor may read it and say, "Well, we have a few problems here," but when it leaves my desk, my manuscript is the very best that I am capable of producing at that moment.

You must be excruciatingly honest with yourself about your writing. Don't fool yourself into thinking there's not a single word that should be altered; and at the same time, try not to agonize over your choice of words *as* you write, or you'll never experience the sheer pleasure that comes when during the revision process, with fingers flying, you're barely able to get the new words down as fast as they are coming to you.

To me, the final revision is a joy. Once I've got something—anything—down on paper, I can almost immediately see what's wrong with it. I've found it's best to go through what I've written several times, checking a different element each time—pace, action, setting, etc. Otherwise, I get caught up in the story and end up patting myself on the back instead of slashing and reworking.

First, I *scan* rather than *read,* checking what's happening on each page to make sure that the beginning is not too slow, too choked with information. I try to see where the novel *actually* starts and where it segues into the middle, and whether the beginning seems to take up too many pages in proportion to the length of the book. I check to be sure the story gets underway with the first sentence.

Is the setting clear? Are the characters presented in a visible and interesting way? Is it obvious which character is doing what?

In the middle I ask myself, "Is anything happening?" If not, I need to go over that page very carefully—not that there has to be some fast and furious action going on, unless it belongs in the story at that point. The action can simply be some important piece of dialogue or two characters meeting for a purpose important to the story. I make sure no one is sitting and musing for long periods of time.

Still in the middle, I check to make sure I have
followed the law of cause and effect and that all
characters' actions are motivated. Is there any
conflict, any suspense? Is the pace O.K.? Will the
reader turn the page? Did the chapter end at an
exciting point so the reader will be eager to go on
to the next chapter?

Next, I consider the ending. Does it seem satisfying, believable, unpredictable, convincingly
motivated? Does every story thread reach a conclusion? Not every conclusion has to be positive,
but it should be satisfying. Is it well motivated?
Believable?

Watch for pace in your ending: Do the explanations drag on endlessly, or does the story end too
quickly? It's O.K., even necessary in most stories,
to tie up the ends, but not too neatly, too easily,
or too rapidly. Otherwise, readers will not have
time to savor the end of your story. If it was going
to be so easy to solve all the problems, they'll wonder, why did it take so long to get to the end?

Let the actions and words of your main characters help the reader see how they have changed.
For instance, the last scene of *Shadow of a Doubt*
shows that the hero and heroine were willing to
compromise. Throughout the story, Turner had
been shown to be a neatness freak. Jamie was
messy. After the mystery is solved, and Jamie and
Turner have admitted their love for one another,
they go to Turner's private beach and undress for
a swim. Turner deliberately tosses each piece of
his clothing onto the sand, letting it fall as it

may—blazer, tailored Bermuda shorts, shirt, tie, shoes, socks. Understanding that he's showing her he's willing to be less fastidious, Jamie removes *her* clothing with dramatic ceremony, folding each piece with exaggerated care and placing it precisely on the edge of Turner's tartan blanket. "Never let it be said I'm not willing to meet a man halfway," she says solemnly.

I tend to be haphazard about time. It's amazing how often I'll find that my heroine has fitted twenty-seven hours of action into a twenty-four-hour day and still had time left over to sleep. This is the kind of thing I fix when I'm revising. If I come across transitions like "It was a busy week," I make sure the calendar I've devised for the novel agrees that a week has passed. Or, if I've written "The roses had faded," I ask myself, How long does it take roses to fade? Is that how much time has passed in the story?

As for transitions, sometimes I decide I don't need one and just leave extra space to indicate a time gap, then start on the next scene. When I decide to keep a transition, I see if it needs cutting, or expanding if it's too abrupt.

It's important to check the characters' clothing. Sometimes I'll find a character isn't dressed appropriately for the action or situation, or I've said, "She smoothed the skirt of her dress," when on the previous page she was wearing pants.

Years ago I worked at a movie studio. It was the job of one woman, known as a continuity *girl* (it was a *long* time ago!) to make sure that when filming was interrupted, then continued on the same set, everything was in the same place as before. The damask napkin that the heroine had flung to the floor could not be back on the table neatly folded when shooting resumed. If the hero was wearing a tie in the last frame, he should be wearing the same tie in the next one. Such details are important to watch for in your writing.

I also check on the weather. If it was raining at the beginning of a particular scene, did the four people in that scene carry umbrellas when they went out, or are they standing around in the street talking, miraculously staying dry?

When I get through with all this trouble-shooting, and I've dealt with the necessary rewriting, I go through the manuscript word by word, rereading from beginning to end with a jaundiced eye, tinkering as I go. What is the purpose of this reading? Still all of the above, but now I'm also making sure I've checked my facts. Am I sure the Jamaica Inn is on Bodmin Moor? Were the ruins of the castle at Tintagel made of slate? Was it definitely Rudyard Kipling who wrote about the smugglers? Did I spell all of the names right?

How does the writing *sound* to me? Are the rhythms right? Are too many sentences cast in the same form? *Jenna answered the doorbell. She opened the door. A woman stood on the doorstep. Jenna looked at her.*

How about the characters. Are they "alive"? Can I visualize them as I read—not just at the beginning, but all the way through? Will the reader care about them, or are they just a bunch of character traits without distinctive personalities?

What about the dialogue? I read some of it aloud if I'm not sure it's right. Mostly, I rely on my *inner* ear. Do all the characters sound alike? Do they *talk* to each other, or do they make speeches? Does anyone go on talking too long, too didactically, too boringly? I edit the dialogue wherever possible, taking out unnecessary comments on the weather, and needless greetings— such as, how-d'you-dos.

Viewpoint. Is it clear whose viewpoint I'm in? Or have I bounced in and out of some minds that would be better left unexplored?

It goes without saying, I hope, that I'm watching for grammatical or spelling errors. I'm also careful about punctuation, though editors may have different styles and terms. I always bow to their preference on this.

Somewhere along the way, I check for word repetitions, to see how many times *well, just,* and *very* jumped in without my noticing. There are usually quite a few that need to be deleted.

Lastly, after all necessary revisions are completed, I read the whole novel again, without stopping, if that's possible. If it still holds my interest, I feel it should hold an editor's and a reader's, as well.

Before a writer sends a manuscript to an editor, it should be the best book he or she can produce. This is the writer's responsibility, the writer's task, the writer's joy.

Checkpoints for Revising Your Novel

Beginning
Did I write in scenes of action, showing rather
than telling?
Is the beginning too slow?
Do the characters begin to come to life
immediately?
Is the setting clear and concise?
Is the beginning interesting?
Have I given too much static information?
Does the story move along?
Is anything happening?

Middle
Did I write in scenes?
Does the story develop in an interesting and
dramatic manner?
Is anything happening?
Are the characters developing, changing, and
growing?
Do the characters act as well as react?
Have I followed the rule of cause and effect?

Ending
Did I write in scenes?
Is the resolution believable? Too predictable?
Too static?
Have the characters changed and grown?
Is the ending too slow? Or too fast?
Have I written beyond the actual ending?
Are the final scenes dramatic and interesting?

General

Have I pruned my words?

Have I used too many adjectives and adverbs?

Have I used strong nouns and active verbs?

Do I have any clichéd characters, situations,
figures of speech?

Is the chronology of the book correct?

Have the people in the novel acted in a
manner consistent with their characters?

Are all transitions clear? And not too long?

Is the viewpoint consistent and clear, or have I
hopped into too many minds?

Will the reader turn every page?

Is something happening?

What is the main conflict? (Conflict does not
necessarily mean argument.)

Have I checked all facts for accuracy?

Can I *feel* the emotions as I read through
(love, hatred, fear, envy, etc.)?

Is the motivation for each action strong and
believable?

Have I edited the dialogue enough?

Have I left any story threads dangling?

Are the spelling and grammar correct?

◄ 12 ►
Marketing Your Novel

Before sending your novel out, there are a few more items you need to check. You have probably given some thought to a title as you wrote, or perhaps even before you began. Sometimes I think of a title as soon as the idea occurs to me. *The Scent of Magic* was one. Other times I write down a working title and hope inspiration will strike somewhere along the way to produce the right one. Usually it does.

None of which means the book will reach the reader with that same title. A publisher may feel that your title won't attract buyers, or is too long, or too difficult to understand. Or perhaps it has been used before. Titles can't be copyrighted, but publishing houses don't like to repeat them for the same kind of work in the same time period.

One of my titles, *The Glass Unicorn,* became *Lovespell; The Singing Trees* turned into *Song of Desire.* Writers often don't like the titles their editors choose, but few have the clout to demand title approval. All the same, if you really dislike a title change made by a publisher, a compromise can often be reached. Whatever the final decision, before you submit your manuscript, it should have a title that you think fits the tone and genre, one that will appeal to prospective readers.

Once you have a title, check your manuscript's physical presentation. Writers vary the format of their manuscripts, but there are some basics:

1. Always double-space.

2. Number pages throughout the entire book, *not* chapter by chapter.

3. Use one- to one-and-a-half-inch margins.

4. The book's title and your name should appear on every page.

5. Include your name, address, and telephone number on the title page, along with the *approximate* word count of your manuscript. If you use a pseudonym, give the publisher *both* your own name and your pen name.

If you are using a computer, justify only the left margin. Justifying the right margin makes spacing peculiar and reading difficult.

Underline words only when you want them set in italics—do not type in italic or bold face. Do not use a dot matrix printer unless it has superb letter-quality print. Dot matrix is very hard to read and editors are put off by it.

If you use a typewriter, be sure the type is dark and legible. Make sure every page is clean and doesn't have globs of correction fluid all over it. Use 20-lb., good-quality paper. Never use erasable paper—it smears.

Don't indicate on the manuscript the rights you are offering. The time for that discussion comes after your book is accepted and the editor offers you a contract.

It is not necessary to apply for copyright for your manuscript; if your book is accepted, the publisher will copyright it *in your name* (this is usually stated in the contract). Nor is it necessary to type copyright information anywhere on your manuscript. According to the law, copyright is secured *automatically* when a work is created in tangible form.

To market your novel, you need to find out as much as you can about the publishing business and how it works. Subscribe to writers' magazines. Join organizations that relate to your field of writing: Mystery Writers of America, Science Fiction Writers of America, Romance Writers of America, the Authors' Guild, and so on. Go to writers' conferences; you will not only learn a lot about writing and publishing, but you'll meet editors and agents and other writers—all of which is helpful and stimulating.

Talk to booksellers. Tell them what kind of book you've written; they may be able to direct you to the publishers who publish similar books. Look at books in the library and bookstores to see who is publishing what. It's a good idea to do this as you are writing your novel. Many authors have a publisher in mind in advance, one whose books they perhaps admire or enjoy reading. Ask publishers for their catalogues, which contain descriptions of the books they publish, season by season.

In the reference department of the library, you will find volumes that list various book publishers—*Literary Market Place*, for instance, which describes briefly the kinds of books each company publishes, how many titles each publishes a year, and so forth. Some, like the annual *The Writer's Handbook*, include longer descriptions of editorial needs, submission procedures, and payment policies.

Make a list of all the publishers most likely to be interested in your type of novel. Then send a query letter or book proposal, depending on submission requirements. I have never approached more than one publisher at a time with a query or book proposal, though this has become an increasingly acceptable approach. Note: Do not send an entire manuscript to a publishing house unless you are asked to do so; it will come winging back to you. And *never* submit an entire manuscript to more than one publisher.

Usually a query letter gets a fairly rapid response. What should be included in a query letter? The title of your novel and its genre—mystery, science fiction, western, romance, whatever. A *brief* description of the storyline. The approximate length. Any publishing credits you already have. The fact that the novel is completed. Ask if you may submit a synopsis and sample chapters.

What should *never* be included in a query letter? Jocular remarks about suicide or starvation or bills piling up. Affidavits stating that friends or relatives tell you you're a great writer. A query letter is a letter from one professional to another.

Always address query letters or proposals to a particular editor by name, which you'll find in the *Literary Market Place*. Or you can make a quick call to the publishing house and ask which editor you should write to about your particular kind of novel. Many publishers will send you guidelines on request; always include a self-addressed stamped envelope (SASE).

When you send a proposal (typically, a synopsis and three sample chapters), package it securely and enclose a self-addressed envelope or label with enough postage for return of the material. I use first-class or priority mail for proposals or complete manuscripts. Manuscript rate is cheaper, but it may take several weeks for a proposal to reach New York—and it may arrive in poor condition. Remember: The way you treat a manuscript says a lot about how important it is to you.

When you mail an entire book manuscript, use a strong cardboard box (the kind a ream of typing paper comes in). I have also wrapped my manuscript in the sturdy white paper that comes off reams of laser printer paper, then put the package in a padded envelope.

Be prepared for rejection. Even if an editor gives you a professional "go-ahead" on your query and asks to see the whole manuscript, he or she may still turn it down.

There are several degrees of rejection. Most common is the printed rejection slip attached to the manuscript. It basically says thanks, but no thanks. Busy editors do not have time to tell you the reasons for turning down a manuscript, unless they think it can be revised to make it acceptable. Nor do they have time to enter into lengthy correspondence with writers whose work they have turned down. Your manuscript might not be right for a particular publishing house. The publisher may have bought a similar novel the week, month, year before, or it just won't fit their list. The first reader may not like it, or thinks it's poorly written.

Don't take rejection personally. In my opinion, the only way to handle rejection is to meet it head on and leap over it. You should never interpret rejection as meaning your manuscript is worthless. Look upon it as a challenge. (I'm going to show *them!*) Nobody's rejecting *you.* If you receive a rejection, it means only that your manuscript did not fit the needs of that particular editor at this particular time. Look at your proposal again to see if you can improve it before sending it out again.

The second degree of rejection includes the editor's comments on the rejection slip. This is usually a good thing to have happen. The editor might not care for this novel but is interested in seeing something from you in the future. Or the comment might say something about the quality of your writing. Even a simple "Sorry!" is encourag-

ing, because it means there was something there
the editor liked. Keep that editor in mind for future projects.

I've only once received a comment on a rejection
slip that was completely negative. I had written
a short mystery story with what I thought was a
really good twist ending and sent it off to a mystery magazine. I became very excited when I saw
a written message on the rejection slip. Until I
read it. "Were we supposed to be surprised?" it
asked. I was crushed.

The third degree of rejection arrives in the form
of a letter telling you why the manuscript is being
turned down. Or it might suggest changes you can
make and ask you to resubmit. *Do it*. But don't
count on a definite sale until you get a definite
offer.

Now for the positive side: Say an editor asks to
see your proposal, likes what you send and also
likes the completed manuscript. If you get a phone
call telling you the editor wants to publish it, your
next order of business will be the publishing
contract.

Don't sign it until you've read it carefully. If
you don't understand parts—and you probably
won't—ask whoever gave you the good news to
explain it to you. If you don't have an agent, or
know a lawyer with experience in literary contracts, ask an established writer to look at the
contract, or try to get an agent on the strength of
the contract.

Once the contract is signed, you will be assigned an editor who will almost certainly request some changes in the manuscript. When that editor is satisfied with the plot and characters and so on, a copy editor will go through the manuscript and make necessary, (and sometimes unnecessary) grammatical and semantic changes.

The novel will be scheduled for publication on a certain date. The publishers may or may not give your novel advance publicity, depending on the custom of that particular house and their advertising budget. You can do a certain amount of publicity yourself by sending out flyers well ahead of publication date to bookstores and to others who can be helpful in promoting your book—libraries, book review editors of magazines and newspapers, for instance. Self-promotion is another book in itself, and your best bet is to wait until you have a contract and then ask other writers in your field what they do. Many writers, even experienced ones, arrange on their own for talks and signings at bookstores in their area.

Now let's talk about editors. I used to think that writers lived on Mount Olympus with all the other gods, and that an editor, on the other hand, was Caesar presiding over the sports arena—a thumb up for life for this gladiator, thumbs down for death for that one.

I have learned that editors are usually quite kindly human beings. I've worked with many, and most have become my friends. But when one of my editors calls me on the telephone and tells me how wonderful my new proposal is and then adds the word I've been waiting for, and dreading— "but. . ."—we are both immediately professional. We know that we both want to produce the best book we can. So my feelings aren't hurt, and I don't take the criticism personally.

After I hang up the phone, I examine my work judiciously and objectively. I might then say, "Nah, what do editors know?" but then I look again and sigh, because I can see that in many cases the editor was right: This part of the plot *is* too thin. On the other hand, when something is changed that I feel strongly about, I fight for it. I've always received a hearing and usually have been allowed to change it back.

All editors are actively looking for good manuscripts. If you have writing talent and are willing to work hard; if you have enough imagination to be original; if you believe that your writing is worth all the talent and skill and care that you can bring to it, then you will find an editor!

Whenever I speak at a conference, I can count on the participants asking certain questions, the most frequently asked being, Should I have an agent?

Answer: Yes.

Of course you should—if and when possible.

Agents are wonderful, often brilliant people. They have to be brilliant to understand publishing contracts and royalty statements. Agents can often get you more money than is first offered, they know who does what and who needs what and who likes what. They socialize with editors. They call them by their first names. They will argue with editors about terms and/or editorial changes if necessary so that you don't ever have to.

However, agents cannot sell something that isn't any good to start with.

Second most-asked question: How can I get an agent?

Ah, yes; now we have a problem. A writer must accept reality. Writing is an art, a craft, a profession. It is also a business. Getting an agent—a literary representative—is rather like getting a bank loan. You must first prove you don't need one. In other words, you need to sell some of your work by yourself, study the markets, learn who does what and who needs what and who likes what. All by yourself. This is very good for a writer's character—but it can be hard on your nerves, and it takes time.

Agents are business people. Their income is based on 10% to 15%—usually the latter—of their authors' income. Because of this, they can afford to take on as clients only those writers who they think have the potential to write salable material. This is good business. It's also common sense.

In my case, after I had sold some thirty or so articles and short stories to minor markets, I sold a children's book. Before signing the contract, I approached an agent with that contract in hand and asked her to represent me. She said yes and helped me sell two more children's books, some short stories to a major magazine, and my first novel.

Unfortunately, shortly after selling my novel, she died. For some time after that, I submitted my manuscripts directly to publishers myself and sold three novels in one go. The advances however, were miserable. (An advance is an amount of money advanced to the writer by the publisher, usually half on signing of the contract, half on delivery of a satisfactory manuscript. It is an *advance* against royalties. If you receive a $2,000 advance and your book sells for $10 and you get 6% royalties—60¢ for each copy sold—then your book will have to sell 3,333 copies before you receive any more money.)

I discovered I was not a good negotiator, so I began to look for another agent. By this time I knew the names of several agents, one of whom had always been spoken of with great respect.

I often read advice to beginning writers suggesting that they ask other writers for the name of *their* agents, and maybe even ask for a personal recommendation. This may be O.K. if those "other writers" have read your work and are wildly enthusiastic about it. But if they are not familiar with your writing, or with you, they're usually very protective of their agents. Since my feeling has always been that I want an agent who likes *my* work, I wrote the agent myself, listing my credits and asking if I could submit a sample of my work. She said yes, I sent in a synopsis and sample chapter of my work in progress, and she took me on as a client. That was about sixteen years ago and I've been contentedly working with her ever since.

Once you've had some writing success and experience, one way of interesting an agent in your work is to set up an appointment with an agent at a writers' conference. Alternatively, you can check lists of agents in *Literary Market Place* and *The Writer's Handbook,* or write for a list of members to The Association of Authors' Representatives Inc., 10 Astor Pl., 3rd Floor, New York, NY 10003. Include a legal-size SASE (with postage-sufficient for two ounces) and a $7 check or money order.

I'll close this chapter, and this book, with three very short stories.

The first, which I've always hoped was apocryphal, deals with a famous writer who was asked to speak at a writing seminar. He stood up in front of the microphone and said, "How many of you want to be writers?" All the hands went up and the famous writer said, "Then go home and write," and sat down.

The second story I *know* is apocryphal because I made it up. It concerns a young man who graduated from MIT and decided he didn't want to be an engineer after all; he wanted to be a violinist. He hadn't ever played an instrument, but he thought Itzhak Perlman made it look pretty simple. So he went to a music store and bought a violin and came home, tuned the strings, put rosin on the bow, tucked the violin under his chin and played the "Intermezzo" from *Cavalleria Rusticana*.

The third story is about the Greek geometrician and mechanician, Archimedes, who once lowered his body into a filled bathtub, spilled water onto the floor, then jumped out and ran naked through the streets of Athens yelling "Eureka!" He had discovered the law of hydrostatics, which states that a body surrounded by a fluid is buoyed up by a force equal to the weight of the fluid it displaces.

It seems to me that the first two stories say the same thing; if you want to do something enough, all you have to do is go home and do it. I don't believe this for a minute.

The third story tells the truth. Archimedes was visited by inspiration, yes, but only after he had devoted his entire life to research and experiment in plane and solid geometry, arithmetic and mechanics. In short, Archimedes had studied his subject. Fortune favors the prepared mind.

It is my hope that this book will help to prepare *you* for the writing of your novel, so that you will know what to do when inspiration strikes. Or doesn't strike.

For several years before I actually wrote a novel, I dreamed of doing it. Because I suspect it has long been *your* dream, I offer this final thought for you to ponder.

If the pursuit of your dream seems endless, if you receive more rejection than encouragement, bear in mind two very important words that were given to us by the ancient Romans: *Nil Desperan-*

dum, which very loosely translated means, hang in there. Pursue your dream actively and professionally, studying, learning, writing, rewriting, looking at your work with complete, maybe even brutal, honesty.

And don't give up. Don't ever give up.